NATIONAL VOTER REGISTRATION ACT

ELEMENTS, ANALYSIS AND IMPACT (WITH ACCOMPANYING CD-ROM)

AMERICAN POLITICAL, ECONOMIC, AND SECURITY ISSUES

Additional books in this series can be found on Nova's website
under the Series tab.

Additional e-books in this series can be found on Nova's website
under the e-book tab.

AMERICAN POLITICAL, ECONOMIC, AND SECURITY ISSUES

NATIONAL VOTER REGISTRATION ACT

ELEMENTS, ANALYSIS AND IMPACT (WITH ACCOMPANYING CD-ROM)

AALIYAH GARNER
EDITOR

publishers
New York

Library of Congress Cataloging-in-Publication Data

ISBN: 978-1-63117-829-0

Published by Nova Science Publishers, Inc. † New York

CONTENTS

PREFACE

After the passage of the Voting Rights Act of 1965, legislation had been urged for over two decades to create a national voter registration system designed to make registration easier and more uniform from state to state. The National Voter Registration Act of 1993, the so-called "motor-voter" bill, was signed into law by President Clinton on May 20, 1993. It required states to establish voter registration procedures for federal elections so that eligible citizens might apply to register to vote simultaneously while applying for a driver's license, by mail, and at selected state and local offices that serve the public. This book provides the history, the implementation and the effects the National Voter Registration Act of 1993. It also discusses the Uninformed Citizens Absentee Voting Act.

Chapter 1 – After the passage of the Voting Rights Act of 1965 (42 U.S.C. §1973–1973aa-6), legislation had been urged for over two decades that would create a national voter registration system designed to make registration easier and more uniform from state to state. The National Voter Registration Act of 1993 (NVRA, P.L. 103-31, 107 Stat.77, [42 U.S.C. §1973gg et seq.]), the so-called "motor-voter" bill, was signed into law by President Clinton on May 20, 1993. It required states to establish voter registration procedures for federal elections so that eligible citizens might apply to register to vote (1) simultaneously while applying for a driver's license, (2) by mail, and (3) at selected state and local offices that serve the public. The law took effect on January 1, 1995, for most states.

Proponents argued that the NVRA would make it easier to register to vote, provide more-than-adequate measures to prevent voter fraud by making violations a federal offense, and cost states very little to implement, based on the experiences of states that previously used some form of "motor-voter" registration.

Opponents, on the other hand, argued that there was little evidence that increasing the number of persons on voter registration rolls would lead to higher voter turnout. By making it so easy to register, they believed the act would increase the likelihood of election fraud. Furthermore, according to opponents, implementation would be costly to the states, in terms both of dollars and other administrative costs.

The NVRA has been the law of the land for over 20 years and has been in effect for 18 years. Between 1992 and 2012, voter registration increased nationally by over seven percentage points. The courts have resolved many of the initial issues. A review of the required NVRA reports appears to indicate that the states have come to terms with the provisions, despite the fact that they would still like the federal government to provide funding for the implementation of aspects of the act. While amending parts of the NVRA in minor ways, the Help America Vote Act, passed in 2002, also created additional voter registration demands on the states (HAVA, P.L. 107-252 [42 U.S.C., Subchapter III, Part A., §15482(a), 15483]).

However, there are still some problems with implementation at the local levels and in some selected state agencies, as well as with the training of non-election officials who are responsible under the NVRA for providing voter registration services. Some would like to curtail parts of the NVRA. Some do not think the NVRA has gone far enough. Proposed legislation introduced in the 113th Congress to deal with various aspects of the voter registration process includes, among others, H.R. 12, H.R. 97, H.R. 280, H.R. 289, and H.R. 2115. This report provides an historical background for voter registration reform and the NVRA, a description of the major aspects of the act, a discussion of the implementation and post-implementation actions, and a catalog of subsequent efforts to amend or repeal the act.

Chapter 2 – This report to the United States Congress addresses the impact of the National Voter Registration Act (NVRA) of 1993 on the administration of elections for Federal office for the 2012 election cycle, i.e., the two-year period following the November 2010 elections through the November 2012 presidential election.

The 2012 report is based on the results of a survey of all States, the District of Columbia, and three territories—American Samoa, Guam, and Puerto Rico—conducted by the Election Assistance Commission (EAC). The U.S. Virgin Islands did not respond to the 2012 survey.

As with past reports, the quality and completeness of responses from many States and territories varied significantly.

Six States and all territories are exempt from the provisions of the NVRA. Other States did not collect voter registration data in a way that was compatible with a few of the survey questions. Jurisdictions in a few States faced challenges in collecting the data, hampering the States' abilities to provide complete data for all jurisdictions.

The survey shows that the number of registered voters increased during the 2012 election cycle. There were approximately 194.2 million total registered voters reported for the November 2012 presidential election, an increase of over 7.3 million registered voters from the 2010 elections. It is important to note that Puerto Rico did not hold Federal elections in 2010. As such, the 2.4 million reported registrations in Puerto Rico contribute to this overall increase in registration. The number of registered voters in 2012 represents an increase of approximately 3.7 million voters since the 2008 presidential election cycle.

According to the responses to the survey and population estimates from the U.S. Census Bureau, 87.4% of American citizens of voting age (18 years or older) were registered to vote in the 2012 elections.

Five States reported a large increase in active registrants compared to the previous presidential election held in 2008, while five States reported a dramatic decrease. Since the previous presidential election, the District of Columbia, South Carolina, and Ohio reported an increase of over 10% in the number of active registrants, and Hawaii and Mississippi indicated an increase of over 20%; Michigan and Nebraska reported a decrease of over 10%, and New Mexico, New York, and South Dakota reported a decrease of over 20%. Active registrants refers to all registered voters except those who have been sent, but who have not responded to a confirmation mailing sent in accordance with NVRA (42 U.S.C. 1973gg-6(d)) and have not since offered to vote.

Chapter 3 – Members of the uniformed services and U.S. citizens who live abroad are eligible to register and vote absentee in federal elections under the Uniformed and Overseas Citizens Absentee Voting Act (UOCAVA, P.L. 99-410) of 1986. The law was enacted to improve absentee registration and voting for this group of voters and to consolidate existing laws. Since 1942, a number of federal laws have been enacted to assist these voters: the Soldier Voting Act of 1942 (P.L. 77-712, amended in 1944), the Federal Voting Assistance Act of 1955 (P.L. 84-296), the Overseas Citizens Voting Rights Act of 1975 (P.L. 94-203; both the 1955 and 1975 laws were amended in 1978 to improve procedures), and the Uniformed and Overseas Citizens Absentee Voting Act of 1986. The law is administered by the Secretary of Defense, who delegates that responsibility to the director of the Federal Voting Assistance Program (FVAP) at the Department of Defense (DOD).

Improvements to UOCAVA were necessary as the result of controversy surrounding ballots received in Florida from uniformed services and overseas voters in the 2000 presidential election. The National Defense Authorization Act for FY2002 (P.L. 107-107) and the Help America Vote Act of 2002 (P.L. 107-252) both included provisions concerning uniformed services and overseas voting. The Ronald W. Reagan Defense Authorization Act for FY2005 (P.L. 108-375) amended UOCAVA as well, and the John Warner National Defense Authorization Act for FY2007 (P.L. 109-364) extended a DOD program to assist UOCAVA voters.

In the 111th Congress, a major overhaul of UOCAVA was completed when President Obama signed the National Defense Authorization Act for FY2010 (P.L. 111-84) on October 28, 2009. It included an amendment (S.Amdt. 1764) that contained the provisions of S. 1415, the Military and Overseas Voter Empowerment Act (the MOVE Act).

In July 2013, the Election Assistance Commission issued its report on UOCAVA voting in the general election of 2012. The biennial report is mandated by the Help America Vote Act. According to the results, ballots were transmitted to UOCAVA voters by election officials in all 50 states and several territories, but nearly half of all ballots were sent from California, Florida, New York, Texas, and Washington. The rate of ballots returned for counting was higher than in 2010, but lower than in the presidential election of 2008. States counted 95.8% of the ballots that were returned.

Several relevant bills have been introduced in the 113th Congress, including H.R. 12, H.R. 1655, H.R. 2168, H.R. 3576, S. 123, S. 1034, and S. 1728. The Senate Committee on Rules and Administration held a hearing on S. 1728 on January 29, 2014.

In: National Voter Registration Act   ISBN: 978-1-63117-829-0
Editor: Aaliyah Garner   © 2014 Nova Science Publishers, Inc.

Chapter 1

THE NATIONAL VOTER REGISTRATION ACT OF 1993: HISTORY, IMPLEMENTATION, AND EFFECTS[*]

Royce Crocker

SUMMARY

After the passage of the Voting Rights Act of 1965 (42 U.S.C. §1973–1973aa-6), legislation had been urged for over two decades that would create a national voter registration system designed to make registration easier and more uniform from state to state. The National Voter Registration Act of 1993 (NVRA, P.L. 103-31, 107 Stat.77, [42 U.S.C. §1973gg et seq.]), the so-called "motor-voter" bill, was signed into law by President Clinton on May 20, 1993. It required states to establish voter registration procedures for federal elections so that eligible citizens might apply to register to vote (1) simultaneously while applying for a driver's license, (2) by mail, and (3) at selected state and local offices that serve the public. The law took effect on January 1, 1995, for most states.

Proponents argued that the NVRA would make it easier to register to vote, provide more-than-adequate measures to prevent voter fraud by making violations a federal offense, and cost states very little to implement, based on

---

[*] This is an edited, reformatted and augmented version of a Congressional Research Service publication, CRS Report for Congress R40609, dated September 18, 2013.

the experiences of states that previously used some form of "motor-voter" registration.

Opponents, on the other hand, argued that there was little evidence that increasing the number of persons on voter registration rolls would lead to higher voter turnout. By making it so easy to register, they believed the act would increase the likelihood of election fraud. Furthermore, according to opponents, implementation would be costly to the states, in terms both of dollars and other administrative costs.

The NVRA has been the law of the land for over 20 years and has been in effect for 18 years. Between 1992 and 2012, voter registration increased nationally by over seven percentage points. The courts have resolved many of the initial issues. A review of the required NVRA reports appears to indicate that the states have come to terms with the provisions, despite the fact that they would still like the federal government to provide funding for the implementation of aspects of the act. While amending parts of the NVRA in minor ways, the Help America Vote Act, passed in 2002, also created additional voter registration demands on the states (HAVA, P.L. 107-252 [42 U.S.C., Subchapter III, Part A., §15482(a), 15483]).

However, there are still some problems with implementation at the local levels and in some selected state agencies, as well as with the training of non-election officials who are responsible under the NVRA for providing voter registration services. Some would like to curtail parts of the NVRA. Some do not think the NVRA has gone far enough. Proposed legislation introduced in the 113th Congress to deal with various aspects of the voter registration process includes, among others, H.R. 12, H.R. 97, H.R. 280, H.R. 289, and H.R. 2115. This report provides an historical background for voter registration reform and the NVRA, a description of the major aspects of the act, a discussion of the implementation and post-implementation actions, and a catalog of subsequent efforts to amend or repeal the act.

RECENT EVENTS

On June 30, 2013, the Election Assistance Commission released the 10th biennial report on the impact of the National Voter Registration Act of 1993 on the 2011-2012 election cycle.

On June 17, 2013, the United States Supreme Court, by a vote of 7-2, held that the National Voter Registration Act of 1993 preempts the state of Arizona law requiring proof of citizenship as part of the voter registration process for those individuals using the "Federal Form," *Arizona, et. al. v. The Inter Tribal Council of Arizona, Inc. et. al., No. 12-71, June 17, 2013.*[1]

On June 4, 2013, the House Committee on House Administration held a hearing on the Voter Registration Efficiency Act (H.R. 2115). The bill is intended to reduce the number of voters registered in multiple states, among other things. The bill would amend the National Voter Registration Act of 1993 to require individuals registering to vote in a state to indicate if the state will be the individual's residence for the purpose of voting and for other purposes.

BACKGROUND

Efforts to establish a national voter registration system followed closely on the heels of passage of the Voting Rights Act in 1965. In the early 1970s, a substantial effort was made to establish a national "postcard" or mail registration system. In the 92nd Congress, both the Senate and the House held hearings on a proposal to establish a national voter registration system, with the Census Bureau conducting postcard registration for federal elections. The proposal came to the Senate floor for a vote but was tabled. In the 93rd Congress, both the Senate and the House again considered much the same proposal; a national postcard voter registration system, administered by a new National Voter Registration Administration located in the Census Bureau. The Senate passed the bill (S. 352, S. Rept. 93-91) on May 9, 1973 (vote: 57-37). The House, on May 8, 1974, refused to take up the bill (H.R. 8053, H. Rept. 93-778) to establish a national postcard voter registration system by rejecting the rule under which the measure was to be debated on the floor (vote:197-204). In 1975, the House passed a modified version of the postcard voter registration measure, eliminating the required mass mailing of postcards to every household; the postcards were to be made available at post offices and other public offices (H.R. 11552; August 9, 1975, H. Rept. 94-798, vote: 239-147). The measure, however, stalled in the Senate.

During the first year of the Carter presidency, reform efforts focused on passage of a national voter registration standard that would have allowed citizens to register to vote on election-day (H.R. 5400, H. Rept. 95-318). Although the proposal initially received strong support, negative reactions from local election officials appear to have caused support to erode. The House version never came up for a vote on the floor. Like the House version, the Senate bill (S. 1072, S. Rept. 95-171) was reported out of committee but never came up for a vote. By mid-1977, election-day voter registration was essentially defeated, and there was little or no effort to revive it for the rest of the Carter presidency.

Between 1983 and 1988 various measures to reform voter registration were proposed. Some proposals would have established a national voter registration system based on postcard registration or election -day registration, or both. Some bills proposed providing financial incentives to the states to encourage a more uniform and open registration system. But, while some hearings on voter registration reform were held during the period, no measure ever reached the floor of either the Senate or the House.

While various bills proposing voter registration reform were introduced during the early 1980s, election reform efforts became more narrowly focused. In 1984, Congress passed the Voting Accessibility for the Elderly and Handicapped Act (P.L. 98-435, 98 Stat. 1678). The act established national requirements for making polling places accessible to the elderly and the handicapped. In addition, the act required each state to provide "a reasonable number of accessible permanent registration facilities," to "make available registration and voting aids for federal elections for handicapped and elderly individuals," and to require "no notarization or medical certification ... of handicapped voters with respect to an absentee ballot or application for such ballot." The act was signed into law September 28, 1984.

In 1986, Congress passed and the President signed the Uniformed and Overseas Citizens Absentee Voting Act (UOCAVA) (P.L. 99-410, 100 Stat. 924). Among other things, the act required the creation of an official postcard form containing a voter registration and absentee ballot application, required each state to "permit absentee uniformed services voters and overseas voters to use absentee registration procedures and to vote by absentee ballot" in all federal elections, and required states to "permit overseas voters to use federal write-in absentee ballots in general elections for federal office" except when the state provides a state absentee ballot approved by the presidential designee and made available at least 60 days in advance of the election. The act was signed into law August 28, 1986.[2]

Both P.L. 98-435 and P.L. 99-410 established national voter registration and election standards. Perhaps considered modest by some, these two acts established a much stronger federal presence in state electoral activities than had been the case in the past.

National Voter Registration Reform

Voter turnout in the 1988 presidential election reached its lowest point in 40 years, just slightly more than 50% of the voting-age population. Partly in response to the turnout trends and partly as a continuation of the long-standing efforts by proponents of registration reform, at the beginning of the 101st Congress, several bills were introduced to reform voter registration procedures. For some supporters, these efforts aimed at completing what had been started by the Voting Rights Act of 1965 and its amendments, eliminating the final barriers to voting: voter registration restrictions. For others, the belief that making it easier to register would encourage more voter participation was the driving force behind support for voter registration reform.

The first "motor-voter" bill was introduced by Representatives Swift and Annunzio in the 101st Congress (H.R. 15 and later reintroduced with modifications by Representative Foley as H.R. 2190, H. Rept. 101-243).[3] In the Senate, Senator Ford introduced the companion bill to H.R. 2190, S. 874 (S. Rept. 101-140). In the House, H.R. 2190 received bipartisan support, with Representative Thomas, then ranking Member of the Subcommittee on Elections, and Representative Gingrich, then minority whip, both sponsors of the bill. H.R. 2190 passed the House February 6, 1990 (vote: 289-132) but was never brought up in the Senate.

S. 250, the National Voter Registration Act of 1991, was introduced in the Senate by Senators Ford and Hatfield in the 102nd Congress. S. 250 differed from the "motor-voter" bill introduced in the 101st Congress (H.R. 2190) and did not receive the same level of bipartisan support. S. 250 passed in the Senate (May 20, 1992, S. Rept. 102-60, vote: 61-38) and in the House (June 16, 1992, vote: 268-153) but was vetoed by President George H. W. Bush.

The provisions of S. 250 were reintroduced at the beginning of the 103rd Congress as H.R. 2 by Representative Swift and as S. 460 by Senator Ford (S. Rept. 103-6). The House passed H.R. 2 on February 4, 1993 (H. Rept. 103-9, vote: 259-160). The Senate passed H.R. 2 with some amendments March 17, 1993, by a vote of 62-37. On May 5, 1993, the House voted on the conference report (Conf. Rept. 103-66, vote: 259-164). The Senate adopted the conference report on May 11, 1993 (vote: 62-36). On May 20, 1993, President Clinton signed the National Voter Registration Act of 1993 into law (P.L. 103-31 [42 U.S.C. §1973gg et seq.]).

The National Voter Registration Act of 1993: Major Provisions

The National Voter Registration Act of 1993 (NVRA, P.L. 103-31 [42 USC §1973gg et seq.]), the so-called "motor-voter" law, required that, for federal elections, states must establish procedures so that eligible citizens may register to vote:

> "(1) by application made simultaneously with an application for a motor vehicle driver's license ... ;
> (2) by mail application ... ; and
> (3) by application in person (A) at the appropriate registration site designated with respect to the residence of the applicant in accordance with state law; and (B) at a federal, state, or nongovernmental office designated under Section 7 (required for state agencies providing public assistance and agencies primarily engaged in providing services to persons with disabilities)." (Sec. 4(a)(1)-(3))

States that had no voter registration requirement (North Dakota) or that allowed citizens to register to vote at polling places on election day, statewide (Minnesota, Wisconsin, and Wyoming), were exempted from the act. This exemption was also applied to New Hampshire and Idaho, which adopted election-day voter registration after the date specified in the original bill language, March 11, 1993. The cut-off date required for state election-day registration was changed (to August 4, 1994) in an amendment contained in P.L. 104-99, passed and signed into law January 26, 1996.

Some suggested that the law would transfer voting registration authority from local election authorities within a state to other state and local agencies. According to proponents, the law required other agencies to make available voter registration forms and materials and to collect completed applications for registering to vote. Only appropriate state election officials, proponents argued, determined whether applications were adequate and, if so, registered the applicants.[4]

With respect to simultaneous application for voter registration and application for a motor vehicle driver's license (the "motor-voter" provision), the law covered new applications, renewals, and changes in address for drivers' licenses. Under the law, an application (or renewal) for a motor vehicle driver's license also served as an application for voter registration for federal elections, unless the applicant failed to sign the voter registration application (§5(a)(1)). The voter registration application form was to be a part of the motor vehicle license application form, but would not require any information that duplicated information required in the driver's license portion of the form (§5(c)(2)). The form could ask for only the minimum amount of information to prevent duplicate registrations and to enable state election officials to determine the eligibility of the applicant and to administer voter registration laws. Further, the law required that the form include a statement that listed each eligibility requirement (including citizenship), contained an attestation that applicants meet each requirement, and required the signature of the applicants, under penalty of perjury. The form also had to include a statement about penalties for the submission of a false voter registration application and a statement that information about either the declination or the office where the citizen registered would remain confidential. Similar language was required on the mail registration form (§9(b)). Proponents of P.L. 103-31 considered the "motor-voter" provisions to be the most important of the three procedures. Proponents expected that most voter registration eventually would occur via motor vehicle driver's license applications.[5] Mail and agency registration were included to provide means for persons who did not normally acquire a driver's license.

P.L. 103-31 required the states to accept and use a mail registration application form, as developed by the Federal Election Commission (FEC) (§6(a)(1)).[6] The mail registration application form, like the motor-vehicle form, could require only such identifying information (including the signature of the applicant) and other information (including data relating to previous registration by the applicant) as was necessary for state election officials to determine the eligibility of the applicant and to administer voter registration laws (§9(b)(1)). The state was required to make available mail registration forms to governmental and private entities for distribution, emphasizing availability to nongovernmental voter registration programs (§6(b)). Further, first-time voters who registered by mail might be required to vote in person if the person had not previously voted in that jurisdiction (§6(c)).

Under the NVRA, all state agencies involved in providing public assistance, as well as all offices in the state providing services to persons with disabilities, were to be designated as voter registration agencies (§7(a)). The state also was required to designate other offices within the state as voter registration agencies (might include public libraries, schools, offices of city and county governments, fishing and hunting license bureaus, and unemployment compensation offices). These voter registration agencies were required to distribute mail registration application forms to service applicants along with the agencies' own forms, unless the applicants declined to register to vote. The agencies were also to provide assistance in the completion of the mail voter registration application if requested. The agencies were not to attempt to influence applicants to register to vote in a certain way or to discourage the applicants from applying to register to vote. The designated agencies were also required to accept completed voter registration forms for transmittal to the appropriate state election official. Transmittal of completed forms was to occur not later than 10 days after the date of receipt or, if accepted within five days before the end of registration for an election, the application was to be transmitted to an election official not later than five days after receipt (§7(d)). Also, U.S. armed forces recruitment offices located within the state were designated as voter registration agencies under the NVRA (Sec.7(c)). In 1998, Congress passed and the President signed H.R. 6, the Higher Education Amendments of 1998. The bill, as signed into law, contained a provision that required institutions of higher learning in states covered by the NVRA to make "a good faith effort to distribute a mail voter registration form ... to each student enrolled in a degree or certified program." (See H.R. 6 §489(b), P.L. 105-244, H.Rept. 105-481, H.Rept. 105-750.)

The NVRA required that, upon receipt and approval or disapproval by the appropriate state election official, each applicant would be sent a notice as to the disposition of the application (§8(a)(2)). A voter registrant's name was not to be removed from the voter registration list except at the request of the applicant, by reason of criminal conviction or mental incapacity, by the death of the applicant, or by the applicant moving out of the jurisdiction (§8(a)(3)-(4)).[7] Registered voters could not be removed from the list for nonvoting (§8(b)(2)). A state's efforts at maintaining up-to-date voter registration rolls were to be conducted in a "uniform, nondiscriminatory" fashion and had to be in "compliance with the Voting Rights Act of 1965" (§8(b)(1)). A state could use the U.S. Postal Service's "National Change Of Address" program to help maintain accurate voter registration rolls (§8(c)(1)). A state could remove a person from its registration list if the registrant notified the election office that he/she had moved or if the registrant failed to respond to a notice sent by the registrar and failed to vote or appear to vote in two federal general elections (§8(d)(1)). That is, the registrant must respond to the notice within the period covered by two general elections—voting being a means of response.[8]

P.L. 103-31 provided no funding to the states to carry out any of the prescribed features. The states could avail themselves of reduced postal rates for mailing for voter registration purposes (Section 8(h)). However, the U.S. Postal Service has stated that receipt of the reduced postal rates also meant a corresponding reduction in level of service. The FEC was to develop, in cooperation with the states, a mail registration form and to provide reports to

Congress every two years on the impact of the act (§9(a)).[9] Both the attorney general and any aggrieved citizen could seek relief under the act. If, after notification, the appropriate state election official failed to carry out the provisions of the act, an aggrieved citizen might bring a civil suit in a U.S. district court (§11(a)-(b)). NVRA made a violation of the voter registration procedures as outlined in the law, either by persons or by election officials, a federal offense (§12). The act went into effect January 1, 1995, or, for states that needed to amend their state constitutions (Arkansas, Vermont, and Virginia), January 1, 1996, or 120 days after the amended state constitutions allowed the passage of the supporting legislation, whichever was later.

THE ISSUES, PRO AND CON

Voter Turnout

Many proponents of P.L. 103-31 argued that by making it easier to register eligible citizens, the law would not only increase the number of persons who were registered to vote but also would encourage more voter turnout. They pointed to the fact that usually over 85% of registered citizens vote in general elections, but only about two-thirds of eligible citizens are registered. Proponents marked the fact that over 90% of the voting-age population had a vehicle driver's license or identification card issued by the states. They noted that voter turnout in states that had a form of "motor-voter" registration was higher than in states without "motor-voter" registration. With the simple mechanism of allowing eligible citizens to complete an application to register to vote, proponents argued, the NVRA could easily produce voter registration rates equal to 90% of the voting-age population as compared to the then current registration figures of 65% to 70% of the voting-age population.[10]

Opponents, on the other hand, argued that there was very little evidence that voter turnout would increase even if voter registration increased.[11] They pointed to studies indicating that voter turnout was related to many factors, not just to voter registration procedures. They noted that voter registration reforms in the states had been continuing for many years, that citizens were better educated than in the past, and, still, voter turnout declined.[12] They pointed to almost equal voter turnout in North Dakota and South Dakota in 1992 (67.28% vs. 66.98%, respectively), where North Dakota had no voter registration requirement while South Dakota had one of the stricter registration systems. Since opponents believed that reforming voter registration procedures would lead to only small increases in voter turnout, they described the NVRA as legislation in search of a purpose, with one critic referring to the bill as "auto - fraudo."[13] And after being in effect for 18 years, the available statistics (1996-2012) indicate that, while voter turnout has increased some, it is still not clear that the act has had a significant impact on voter turnout (see "The Response of the Citizenry" section, below).

Voting Rights

Proponents of the NVRA argued that it was necessary to prevent discriminatory and restrictive procedures that disproportionately affected minorities, the poor, the elderly, and the disabled. Some of these proponents viewed the NVRA as a necessary extension of the Voting Rights Act of 1965 to eliminate those barriers to voting still experienced by minorities. They argued that each citizen had a right to vote and that voter registration procedures should not be used to test the fortitude and determination of citizens wanting to vote. Although there were legitimate administrative reasons for requiring citizens to register, these proponents argued, the process itself should not discourage citizens from becoming involved in elections. Incorporating voter registration into the drivers' licensing process provided a secure and convenient method for registering voters, proponents contended.[14] Opponents argued, however, that in most states the voter registration procedures were not burdensome and that many states were moving to more efficient and easier systems all the time; 23 states and the District of Columbia already had a form of motor-voter registration prior to the passage of NVRA. Consequently, they claimed, the federal government did not need to pass legislation mandating that each state register voters in the same way. Voter registration administration had traditionally been within the state's purview, opponents stated, and there was little reason to change it.[15]

Costs of Implementation

Opponents argued that the NVRA imposed on the states an expensive, burdensome procedure that was not necessary. For example, 10 states estimated their combined costs for the NVRA would be $87.55 million, and a representative of the California County Clerks' Election Legislation Committee testified that the bill would cost California $26 million per year and the nation between $200 million and $250 million per year.[16] Further, opponents noted that the extra time spent in assisting applicants to register to vote in public assistance offices and in offices serving the disabled was likely to mean that fewer of these needy persons would be served adequately.[17]

Proponents argued that the cost figures from states that currently had "motor -voter" registration systems suggested that the costs would be between $0.03 and $0.33 per new registrant.[18] They also pointed out that many estimates used by opponents were based on costs associated with adding the larger number of new registrants, not the costs of implementing "motor - voter." Further, these proponents argued, allowing voter registration to occur over the full election cycle would even out the work of voter registration throughout the period. Also, they noted that the Congressional Budget Office estimated that the proposals (S. 250) would have cost all states between $20 million and $25 million a year for the first five years of the program.[19]

Differences between proponents and opponents of the NVRA with respect to cost estimates were likely due more to estimating the costs of two different sets of policies. First, there were the costs of implementing the policies as set out in the NVRA, the costs of registering citizens. Second, there were costs associated with running elections in the states, which might increase because the number of registered voters increased. Costs associated with successfully implementing the voter registration procedures as specified in the NVRA might not be significantly higher than the costs of currently registering citizens in some states except, possibly, for those costs associated with changes to list maintenance. However, if procedures for running elections were directly tied to the number of registered voters, then costs for running an election could have been significantly higher than was currently the case prior to NVRA. If, as proponents argued, the percentage of the voting-age population who were registered increased from 65% to 90%,[20] almost a 40% change, the impact of the NVRA on running elections might have been significant. However, for whatever reason, this large increase in registered voters has not yet occurred.

Even after being in effect for 18 years, however, there are few cost estimates for the NVRA. In one of its earlier reports to Congress, the FEC dismissed the idea that a cost estimate was even possible.

A few people, during the rulemaking process, urged the FEC to collect data regarding the costs of the NVRA. But for several reasons, there is no practical way of determining what the added costs of the NVRA might be ... the FEC would have had to rely on estimated costs. And past experience suggests that estimated costs tend to vary inversely with the estimator's opinion of the law in the first place.... In sum, true cost figures are just too murky.[21]

The report suggests two reasons for the difficulty to develop any cost estimates: (1) the nature of the budgeting process at the local level (most local offices cannot estimate their total election costs much less the costs of a change in voter registration procedures); and, (2) the differential impact of NVRA on the states. Some states already had many of the procedures required while others had none.[22]

The report does go on to point out that the increased mailing costs resulting from the requirements of the NVRA would be what the local election officials would have to bear the most, and this was likely to be substantial. Nationally, this would require:

- quadrennial verification mailings to a minimum of 186 million people
- biennial confirmation mailings to a minimum of 10 million people
- biennial return postage on confirmation postcards from a minimum of 2 million people, and
- biennial acknowledgement mailing to a minimum of 40 million people.[23]

The report notes that the "total postage costs (not to mention printing and handling costs) have now become and will continue to be a major item in every registrar's budget."[24]

U.S. PIRG, a coalition of state public interest research groups (see http://www.uspirg.org/about-us), released a study in 2009 of 100 counties of various sizes in 36 states that estimated that the cost to conduct registration and run error-correction programs on the voter registration information was $33,467,910 for the 2008 election.[25] According to the report, in counties in the survey with populations under 50,000, total expenditures were estimated at $86,977 per county; in counties with population between 50,000 and 200,000 persons, the total expenditures were $248,091 per county; and, in counties with total populations between 200,000 and around 1,000,000, the total expenditures per county were estimated to average $1,079,610.[26] As the report notes, these estimates apply only to the 100 counties included in the survey, and were considered to be "conservative."[27]

Some other findings from the report noted that most registrars estimate that their staffs spend at least 50% of their time working on registration issues, while some indicated a greater proportion of time spent on such work. For offices from the small counties (under 50,000 people), the average cost of employee time on registration was estimated to be almost $ 73,000. For medium-sized counties (50,000-200,000 people), this average cost was estimated to be a little more than $212,000 per office. And for the larger counties (over 200,000 persons), the average cost was estimated to be almost $938,000 for the 2008 election cycle.[28]

Election Fraud

Opponents argued that the NVRA, by making it easier to register to vote and by not providing states with adequate resources to keep their registration lists up -to -date and "clean," opened the door to the possibility of election fraud. And, opponents noted, in those states with large noncitizen populations, the act made it easy for ineligible persons to register to vote. These opponents noted that the process is almost automatic when a person applies for a driver's license, a form of identification that is used by many immigrants to obtain work. The NVRA would be responsible, opponents argued, for the improper voter registration of large numbers of noncitizens.[29]

Proponents argued that P.L. 103-31, by making election fraud a federal offense, strengthened, not weakened efforts to prevent fraud. Proponents noted that many states with mail registration systems required only an attestation of citizenship or other eligibility requirement and a signature under penalty of perjury, as did the NVRA. Nothing in P.L. 103-31 prevented any state, for example, from asking applicants on the combined form whether or not they were citizens.[30] P.L. 103-31, argued proponents, provided sufficient protection against election fraud.[31] This author was unable to find any systematic evidence or empirical study for or against an increase in voter registration fraud as a result of the implementation of the NVRA, nor have the Federal Election Commission (FEC) or the Election Administration Commission (EAC) ever mentioned this as a problem that the states have brought up.[32]

NVRA IMPLEMENTATION

The Federal Response

Under the NVRA, no federal agency is responsible for implementation of the act. Although the FEC (EAC) was responsible for developing the mail registration form and for delivering a report to Congress every two years on the effectiveness of the NVRA, it had no further legal authority under the act. Similarly, the Department of Justice could bring suit against a state for the non-implementation of the law, or for violations as specifically outlined in the NVRA, but had no authority to prescribe state implementation of the law. Implementation is, and has always been, the sole responsibility of each state.

Development of the Mail Voter Registration Form

The FEC printed proposed rules relating to the design and content of the NVRA mail registration form in the *Federal Register* on March 10, 1994 (59 F.R. 11211-11222). After extensive discussions with the states covered by the NVRA, the FEC released the final rules relating to the design and content of the mail registration form on June 23, 1994 (59 FR 32311-32325). Final approval of the form was given by the commission on November 8, 1994.

The form required eight data items: (1) full name of applicant; (2) address where applicant lives; (3) mailing address, if different from where applicant lives; (4) month, day, and year of birth; (5) telephone number (optional); (6) voter identification number, if required by state law; (7) political party preference, if required by state law; and (8) race for states required to collect such data under the Voting Rights Act of 1965 (optional for all other states). In addition, certain information had to be included on the form. Among other items were (1) eligibility requirements (including citizenship); (2) an attestation that the applicant met the state's requirements; (3) a signature and date field; (4) a warning about the penalties for submitting false information; (5) a field for the name and address of anyone who helped the applicant to complete the form; (6) a statement that a refusal to register to vote will remain confidential; and (7) a statement that if the applicant does register, the place of registration remains confidential.

As a result of the passage of the Help America Vote Act of 2002 (P.L. 107-252),[33] the following additions were required to be made to the form (see §303(b)(4)(A)(i-iv)): (1) a question was added specifically asking whether the person registering was a citizen, along with appropriate answer check boxes; (2) a question was added specifically asking whether the person registering to vote was or would be 18 years of age by the next election, again with the appropriate check boxes; (3) a statement was added to the effect that if the person registering to vote had answered "No" to either of the previous questions, then he/she was to stop filling out the form and not register; and (4) a statement was added to the effect that if the completed form was being mailed and the person was registering for the first time, copies of appropriate identification were to be included in the mailing or the person might be required to provide such identification when voting for the first time in the jurisdiction.

Biennial NVRA Report Findings

As a requirement of the NVRA (P.L. 103-31), the FEC (subsequently, the EAC) was responsible for producing a biennial report "assessing the impact of this Act on the administration of elections for federal office ... including recommendations for improvements in Federal and State procedures, forms, and other matters affected by this Act" (§9(a)(3)) . Other than this general mandate, there were no instructions about what specific information was to be included in the reports. As a result, the FEC/EAC chose to conduct surveys of the states to collect the information that the FEC/EAC deemed necessary to complete this mandate.[34]

There have been 10 such reports.[35] With the exception of the first report, each of the NVRA reports provide detailed discussion and statistics on the voter registration activity of the states for each of the periods under study. These include examinations of total voter registration, new registrants, sources of registrations (i.e., motor-vehicle agencies, mail, in-person at election offices, or other designated state office), and list maintenance issues, including removals from lists and reasons for such removals.

On June 30, 1997, the Federal Election Commission, as part of its obligations under the NVRA, released its second report on the impact of the NVRA. The report was based on the responses of 43 states and the District of Columbia. Six states were not included in the survey because they are exempt from the provisions of the act. Vermont was not included because state constitutional impediments had delayed full implementation. The report found that voter registration (as a percentage of the voting-age population) in states covered by the NVRA rose in 1996 by 3.9 percentage points (from 71.7% to 75.6%, or over 12 million people) over 1992, the previous comparable election. During the 22 months the act was in effect, a total of almost 41.5 million registration applications or transactions were processed nationwide. Two-thirds of the registration applications (about 27.5 million) represented new transactions. The duplication rate was 5.2%. The remaining one-third of the total transactions (14 million) represented changes of names and/or addresses. A total of 8.7 million names were deleted from the registration lists, and another 7.0 million were declared "inactive." In addition, the report noted that voter turnout (as a percentage of the voting-age population) declined by five percentage points as compared to 1992.[36]

The mail registration provisions of the NVRA, according to the FEC report, caused relatively few problems for the states and accounted for nearly one-third of all voter registration applications from 1995 through 1996. The motor vehicle provisions proved easiest for the states to implement and yielded the highest volume of registration applications (33.1% or 13.7 million of all registration applications). Applications received at all designated state voter registration agencies represented over 11% of the total number of registration applications in the United States.[37]

The FEC's report made three recommendations:

(1) states, "which do not currently require applicants to provide Social Security numbers", should change election laws to require applicants to provide, at least, the last four digits of their Social Security number and attempt to gather this information for current registered voters;

(2) states, which have not yet done so, should "develop and implement a statewide computerized voter registration database", ensuring that "all local registration offices are computerized" and linking their statewide computerized system with the computer systems of other public agencies relevant to the NVRA; and

(3) the U.S. Postal Service should create a new class of mail for "official election material," providing the most affordable rates for first class treatment.[38]

The third report of the FEC, covering the period 1997-1998, was released June 30, 1999. The report found that in states covered by the NVRA, active voter registration (as a percentage of the voting-age population) rose 7.7 percentage points (from 68.3% to 76.0%) or almost 20 million people, over comparable figures for 1994. During the period, a total of 35.4 million registration applications or transactions were processed nationwide. About half, or 17.6 million, represented new transactions. The duplication rate was 6.5%. The remaining 43.7% of the total transactions (15.5 million) represented changes of names and/or addresses. A total of 9.0 million names were deleted from the registration lists, and another 14.6 million were declared "inactive." In addition, the report noted that voter turnout (as a percentage of the voting-age population) declined by 2.4 percentage points as compared to 1994.[39]

Similar to the 1995-1996 period, the 1997-1998 FEC report noted that the mail registration provisions of the NVRA "caused relatively few problems for the states and accounted for nearly one-quarter of all voter registration applications from 1997 through 1998." Likewise, the motor vehicle provisions proved easiest for the states to implement and yielded the highest volume of registration applications (15.2 million, or 42.9% of all registration applications). Voter registration activity by designated state voter registration agencies accounted for 8.2% (2.9 million) of voter registration applications during the period 1997 through 1998. The FEC made the same three recommendations that it had made in the second report.[40]

The fourth report of the FEC, covering the period 1999 -2000, released June 30, 2001, was based on the survey responses from 44 states and the District of Columbia covered by the NVRA. The report found that in states covered by the NVRA voter registration (as a percentage of the voting-age population) rose by 1.1 percentage points over comparable figures for 1996 (75.6% to 76.7% of the voting-age population). During the period, a total of 45.7 million registration applications or transactions were processed nationwide. About half, or 22.5 million, represented new transactions. The duplication rate was 7.7% (3.5 million). The remaining 43.0% of the total transactions (19.7 million) represented changes of names and addresses. A total of 13.0 million names were deleted from the registration lists, and another 18.3 million were declared "inactive."[41]

Similar to the two earlier periods, the FEC report noted that the mail registration provisions of the NVRA caused relatively few problems for the states and accounted for nearly one-third of all voter registration applications (14.2 million). The registration applications via motor vehicle offices again yielded the highest volume of registration applications (17.4 million, or 38.1% of all registration applications). However, survey results indicated "numerous problems with completed voter registration applications being forwarded from motor vehicle offices to the appropriate election official in a timely manner during the most recent election cycle." Voter registration at designated state voter registration agencies accounted for 7.6% (3.5 million) of voter registration applications.[42]

The FEC again made the same three recommendations that it had made in the two previous reports. The report also added four other recommendations based specifically on the experiences of the 2000 election. These were the following:

(1) "that states develop and implement an on-going, periodic training program for relevant motor vehicle and agency personnel regarding their duties and responsibilities under the NVRA as implemented by the state's law;"

(2) "that states require motor vehicle and agency offices to promptly transmit information regarding voter registration applicants electronically to the appropriate election office with documentation to follow;"

(3) "that states devise a procedure whereby voters may cast a provisional ballot at the polls on election day under circumstances prescribed in state law but at least for the purposes of the fail-safe provisions of the NVRA;" and,

(4) "that states adopt the practice of mailing a forwardable notice to all persons who are removed from the voter registration list whose mail has not previously been returned as undeliverable."[43]

The fifth report of the FEC, covering the period 2001-2002, released June 30, 2003, was based on the survey responses from 44 states and the District of Columbia covered by the NVRA. The report found that in states covered by the NVRA voter registration (as a percentage of the voting - age population) declined by 1.8 percentage points from comparable figures for the last mid-term election in 1998 (76.0% to 74.2% of the voting-age population). During the period, a total of 37.5 million registration applications or transactions were processed nationwide. Over half or 19.7 million represented new transactions. The duplication rate was 8.7%. The remaining 38.7% of the total transactions represented changes of names and addresses. A total of 15.0 million names were deleted from the registration lists, and another 20.6 million were declared "inactive."[44]

Similar to the earlier periods, the FEC report noted that the mail registration provisions of the NVRA caused relatively few problems for the states and accounted for more than one-fourth of all voter registration applications (27.6%). The registration applications via motor vehicle offices again yielded the highest volume of registration applications (42.8% of all registration applications received). Unlike the previous reporting period, survey results indicated a significant decrease in the number of problems reported in the state motor vehicle registration programs, although timeliness in transmitting voter registration application remained a problem.[45] Voter registration at designated state voter registration agencies accounted for 5.8% of voter registration applications.[46]

NVRA Reports two through four, as discussed above, all made the same three core recommendations: (1) states should amend their election laws to use the last four digits of the social security number for all new voter registration applications; (2) states should develop and implement a statewide voter registration database, linking all local offices to a centralized database; and, (3) the United States Postal Service should create a new class of mail for "official election materials" with favorable rates and first class treatments.[47] In addition, NVRA Report 1999-2000 had added four other recommendations: (1) states should develop and implement an on-going, periodic training program for relevant motor vehicle and agency personnel regarding their duties with respect to NVRA; (2) states should require motor vehicle and agency offices to promptly transmit information regarding voter registration applicants electronically to the appropriate election officials; (3) states should develop a procedure for provisional voting, extending or helping to implement better the fail-safe procedures in NVRA; and, (4) states should adopt the procedure of mailing a forwardable notice to all persons removed from voter registration lists.[48] With the exception of the recommendation relating to a special mailing category for NVRA election materials and training programs for state motor vehicle and agency personnel, all of the other FEC recommendations were incorporated, as a whole or in part, in the Help America Vote Act of 2002 (P.L. 107-252). Consequently, the 2001-2002 NVRA Report only repeated the recommendation about the special mailing category and urged the states to set up training programs for state motor vehicle and agency personnel.[49]

The sixth report, and the first report submitted by the newly created EAC, covered the period 2003-2004 and was released June 30, 2005. It was based on the survey responses from 48 states, the District of Columbia, and three of the five territories (American Samoa, Puerto Rico, and the U.S. Virgin Islands). The report found voter registration for states covered by the provisions of the NVRA (as a percentage of the voting-age population) increased by 1.7 percentage points from comparable figures for the last presidential election in 2000 (from 76.7% to 78.4% of the voting-age population). During the period, a total of 49.6 million registration applications or transactions were processed nationwide. Over half (26 million) represented new transactions. Nearly 3.5 million (7.3%) were duplication registrations. About 1.6 million applications (5.2%) were rejected or determined to be invalid. Some 15.2 million of the total transactions represented changes of names and/or addresses. Nearly 12.6 million names were deleted from the registration lists, while another 10.7 million were declared "inactive."[50]

The EAC report noted that the mail registration accounted for almost one-third of all voter registration applications (32.4%). The registration applications received via motor vehicle offices yielded the highest volume of registration applications, but only 32.8% of all registration applications received. The number of registration applications received in person at election or registrar offices amounted to 25.4% of all registration applications. Almost 11% of all registration applications came from designated state voter registration agencies.[51]

The recommendations of the EAC in the sixth report more closely reflected the passage of HAVA's provisions relating to the requirement that each state must establish a statewide voter registration database by January 1, 2006 (P.L. 107 -252, §303(a)(1)(A)), than any provisions specific to NVRA. First, states should provide for electronic transmission of voter registration information from state motor vehicle and other designated NVRA state voter registration agencies directly to local election officials. Second, "states should perform list maintenance through electronic coordination with state and federal databases." The report specifically mentioned the U.S. Postal Service National Change of Address and Social Security Death Index databases, as well as records from U.S. Attorneys and U.S. District Courts concerning criminal conviction records. And third, "states should develop statewide voter registration databases that are capable of tracking a registrant's voting and registration history."[52]

The seventh report covered the period 2005-2006 and was released June 30, 2007. It was based on the survey responses from all states, the District of Columbia, and four territories (American Samoa, Guam, Puerto Rico, and the U.S. Virgin Islands). The report found voter registration for states covered by the provisions of the NVRA (as a percentage of the voting-age population) increased by 2.1 percentage points over comparable figures for the last mid-term election in 2002 (from 74.2% to 76.3% of the voting-age population). During the period, a total of 36.3 million registration applications or transactions were processed nationwide. Nearly half (17.3 million) represented new transactions. Nearly 2.2 million were duplication registrations. Some 10.9 million of the total transactions represented changes of names and addresses. Nearly 13 million names were deleted from the registration lists, while another 9 million were declared "inactive."[53]

The EAC report noted that the mail registration accounted for almost a quarter of all voter registration applications (22.8%). The registration applications received via motor vehicle offices yielded the highest volume of registration applications (45.7% of all registration applications received). The number of registration applications received in person at election or registrar offices amounted to 19.8% of all registration applications. Over 11% of all registration applications came from designated state voter registration agencies.[54]

For the seventh report EAC merged two recommendations and kept one recommendation from its sixth report, as well as added two additional recommendations. The first recommendation merges the first and second recommendations from the 2003-2004 Report and reads, "states should continue to improve and modernize their electronic reporting and list maintenance systems." The second recommendation repeats recommendation three from the 2003-2004 Report. The third recommendation in the 2005-2006 report is a message to the states about standardizing the information needed for the NVRA report to Congress, which reads as follows:

> states should set up their statewide data collection system to facilitate the collection and reporting of information mandated by NVRA. States should work in partnership with the EAC to establish agreed-upon standards for the handling of active and inactive voters, overseas and military voters, and other important categories for the NVRA.

The fourth recommendation in this report is similar to a previous recommendation in the NVRA Report 2001-2002, and reads "states should provide training to all agencies involved in voter registration."[55]

The eighth EAC report covered the period 2007-2008, and was released June 30, 2009. It was based on survey responses from all states, the District of Columbia, and four territories (America Samoa, Guam, Puerto Rico, and the U.S. Virgin Islands). The report found voter registration for states covered by the provisions of the NVRA (as a percentage of the voting-age population) increased by 4.2 percentage points over comparable figures for the last presidential election cycle (2003-2004, from 78.4% to 82.6% of the voting-age population).[56] During the period covered by the report, a total of more than 60 million registration applications or transactions were processed nationwide. Of these, 24.6 million (or over 40%) represented new voters, which were 7.3 million more new voters than had registered in the prior election cycle (2005-2006).[57] More than 20 million of these registration forms requested a change to name, address, or party of the registrant.[58] About 3.6 million applications were determined to be duplicates and another 1.7 million were determined to be invalid or otherwise rejected. Combined, duplicates and invalid registration applications constituted 8.8% of the registration applications for this period. More than 12 million names were deleted from the registration lists, "for reasons including death, felony conviction, failure to vote in consecutive elections, having moved from one jurisdiction to another, or at the voter's request."[59]

The EAC report noted that mail registration accounted for 28.8% of all applications. Registration applications received via motor vehicle offices yielded the highest volume of registration applications, although only slightly above mail registration (30.1% of all registration applications received). The number of registration applications received in person or at election or registrar offices amounted to 14.9% of all registration applications.[60] Over 6% (3,807,991) of all registration applications came from designated state voter registration agencies and 1.1% came through internet applications.[61]

The EAC's eighth report retained one recommendation from its previous report and added five new recommendations. The retained recommendation reads, "states should continue to improve and modernize their electronic reporting and list maintenance systems." Second, the EAC recommends that the "states should explore supporting a coordinated data collection effort that allows local jurisdictions to provide election data to their State election offices." Third, the EAC recommends that "states should provide EAC with information on their proven best practice models of election data collection in order to facilitate sharing with all States through EAC's clearinghouse function." Fourth, the EAC recommends that "states are encouraged to use technology to ease the workload on their election offices, as they deem appropriate." Fifth, the EAC recommends that "states should encourage their public service agencies to remind voters to check and update their registration information." And sixth, the EAC recommends that "for the purpose of compiling comparable election data from future EAC Election Administration and Voting Surveys EAC will continue to work towards a common understanding of election terms."[62]

The ninth report covered the period 2009-2010 and was released June 30, 2011. It was based on survey responses from all states, the District of Columbia and four territories (American Samoa, Guam, Puerto Rico, and the U.S. Virgin Islands). The report found voter registration for states covered by the provisions of the NVRA (as a percentage of the voting age population) increased by 3.2 percentage points over comparable figures for the last non-presidential election cycle (2005-2006, from 76.3% to 79.5% of the voting age population).[63] During the period covered by the report, a total of 45.5 million registration applications or transactions were processed nationwide. Of these, nearly 14.4 million (or over 30%) represented new voters, which was 2.9 million fewer than during the prior comparable election cycle (2005-2006).[64] More than 18 million of these registration forms or transactions requested a change to name, address, or party affiliation of the registrant.[65] About 2.9 million applications were determined to be duplicates and another 1.4 million were determined to be invalid or otherwise rejected. Combined, duplicates and invalid registration applications constituted 9.4% of the registration applications for the 2009 - 2010 election cycle. More than 14 million registrants were deleted from the registration lists "for reasons including death, felony convictions, failure to respond to a confirmation notice and failure to vote in consecutive federal elections (both required under NVRA before a registrant's name can be removed), having moved from one jurisdiction to another, or at the voter's request."[66]

The 2009-2010 EAC report noted that mail registration (mail, fax, and email where permitted) accounted for 20.9% of the 45.5 million voter registration forms. Registration applications received via state motor vehicle agencies yielded the highest volume of registration applications (37.1% of all voter registration applications). The number of registration applications received in-person amounted to 14.5% of all registration applications.[67] Almost 6% (2,541,440) of all registration applications came from designated state voter registration agencies other than state motor vehicle agencies. Internet applications, in those states that allowed such applications (not currently required by NVRA), constituted 1.7% of all applications.[68]

The EAC's ninth report contained no recommendations. This was due to the fact that at the time of the release of the report (required under NVRA), EAC lacked a quorum of commissioners to vote on such recommendations.[69]

The 10th report covered the period 2011-2012 and was released June 30, 2013. It was based on survey responses from all states, the District of Columbia and four territories (American Samoa, Guam, Puerto Rico, and the U.S. Virgin Islands). The report found voter registration for states covered by the provisions of the NVRA (as a percentage of the voting age population) declined by 3.0 percentage points (from 82.6% in the 2007-2008 election cycle to 79.6% in the 2011-2012 election cycle).[70] During the period covered by the report, a total of 62.5 million registration applications or transactions were processed nationwide. Of these, nearly 23.8 million (or over 38%) represented new voters, which was 0.8 million fewer than during the prior comparable presidential election cycle (2007-2008).[71] Almost 27.5 million of these registration forms or transactions requested a change to name, address, or party affiliation of the registrant.[72] Nearly 3.7 million applications were determined to be duplicates and another 5.0 million were determined to be invalid or otherwise rejected. Combined, duplicates and invalid registration applications constituted 13.9% of the registration applications for the 2011-2012 election cycle. Nearly 13.7 million registrants were deleted from the registration lists "for reasons including death, felony convictions, failure to respond to a confirmation notice and failure to vote in consecutive federal elections (both required under NVRA before a registrant's name can be removed), having moved from one jurisdiction to another, or at the voter's request."[73]

The 2011-2012 EAC report noted that mail registration (mail, fax, and email where permitted) accounted for 23.3% of the 62.5 million voter registration forms. Registration applications received via state motor vehicle agencies yielded the highest volume of registration applications (33.4% of all voter registration applications). The number of registration applications received in-person amounted to 16.4% of all registration applications.[74] Over 6% (3,866,542) of all registration applications came from designated state voter registration agencies other than state motor vehicle agencies.[75] Twenty-one states reported voter registration applications by the Internet. Such applications, in those states that allowed such applications (not currently required by NVRA), constituted 5.3% of all applications.[76]

The EAC's 10th report contained no official EAC recommendations. This was due to the fact that at the time of the release of the report (required under NVRA), the EAC lacked a quorum of commissioners to vote on such recommendations. However, the report does offer what are called "observations." First, "states should continue to improve and modernize their electronic reporting and list maintenance systems." Second, "states should continue to engage their State agencies on issues related to the NVRA and to encourage those agencies to remind voters to check and update their voter registration information."[77]

Department of Justice Activity

As of May 1994, 23 states had complied with the NVRA, according to a Department of Justice news release (Alaska, Arkansas, Arizona, Colorado, Connecticut, Delaware, Florida, Georgia, Hawaii, Iowa, Kentucky, Maine, Maryland, Massachusetts, Mississippi, Missouri, Nebraska, Oregon, South Dakota, Tennessee, Utah, Washington, and West Virginia). At that time, Justice officials indicated that enforcement of the NVRA would be one of the department's highest priorities.

On January 22, 1995, the Justice Department filed suit against California, Illinois, and Pennsylvania for failure to implement the NVRA by January 1, 1995. South Carolina was also sued on February 6, 1995. Subsequently, on May 4, 1995, the Justice Department and Pennsylvania agreed that the state would fully implement the NVRA, pending passage of legislation. Both California and Illinois, after having decisions handed down by the respective U.S. Courts of Appeal that ruled against their challenges, implemented NVRA. Also, on April 25, 1995, the Justice Department notified Montana about its failure to implement parts of the NVRA (the state failed to implement agency-based registration and to bring its mail registration form into line with the

NVRA requirements). In a reply letter dated May 4, Montana agreed to correct the oversight. Although Georgia and Texas developed the NVRA proposals and had implemented the NVRA voter registration procedures, the Justice Department challenged aspects of the implementations under provisions of the Voting Rights Act of 1965. Subsequently, these were resolved and both remain in compliance. Differences that the Justice Department had with Louisiana's implementation plan also were resolved, and Louisiana reached full compliance.

During the period 1998-2009, the Justice Department filed suit in five cases brought against three states (New York, Indiana, and Missouri) for failure to implement parts of the NVRA. The three New York cases concerned the designation of state voter registration agencies.[78] Both the Indiana case[79] and the Missouri case[80] concerned the obligations of the state for list maintenance and whether or not the states were in compliance. The remaining suits filed during this period relating to the enforcement or lacks of enforcement of the provisions of NVRA (86 cases)[81] were brought by private persons or organizations. For whatever reason, the Justice Department brought very few suits against the states during this period. Arguably, this was due to the perception that states' enforcement of the provisions of NVRA was adequate, to a lack of resources at the department for such activities, to a policy decision not to exert much effort behind such enforcement, or to a combination of the three.

Recently, there has been criticism of the Justice Department, mainly directed toward the operations under the Bush Administration with respect to enforcement of NVRA. Most of this criticism has been directed at the lack of enforcement of provisions relating to NVRA's agency-based voter registration provisions. In an article authored by Michael Slater, deputy director of Project Vote, he discussed the issue and provided statistics suggesting the lack of state efforts in promoting agency-based voter registration. Slater also argued that "the U.S. Department of Justice has failed to investigate recent allegations that states are not complying with the public agency requirements of the NVRA"[82] However, as noted above, the NVRA reports indicate that, while there was a drop in applications in state voter registration agencies during the period 1997-2002, states reported the same level of applications received from these agencies in the 2003-2004 and 2005-2006 periods as they had received in the 1995-1996 reporting periods. However, the level of applications dropped by almost half from the state agencies during the 2007-2008 reporting cycle.[83]

In hearings in early April 2009, the chairman of the Senate Rules and Administration Committee, Senator Charles Schumer, pressed Attorney

General Eric Holder to "pull out all the stops" and sue any state not complying with the agency-based provisions of the NVRA. In a statement, Senator Schumer noted that "this law is supposed to simplify the voter registration process, but it has been complicated by the rogue behavior of a large batch of states."84 There is some evidence that even before the criticisms, the Department of Justice had made moves to enforce these provisions of the NVRA.[85]

The Response of the States

Overall, responses from most states were cooperative and, despite misgivings about the costs, aimed at the implementation of the NVRA by the January 1, 1995, deadline. However, a few states decided to avoid or challenge the NVRA.

As explained earlier, the provisions of the NVRA were not applicable to states that had had no voter registration system on or before March 11, 1993 (North Dakota), that had had an election-day voter registration procedure at every polling place in effect on or before March 11, 1993 (Minnesota and Wisconsin), or had made the adoption of an election-day registration system contingent on the passage of the NVRA (Wyoming). In an attempt to avoid the implementation of the provisions of the NVRA, which were viewed as costly, Idaho, in January 1994, and New Hampshire, in March 1994, passed legislation adopting election-day voter registration and made it retroactive as of March 11, 1993. Congress effectively ratified this strategy when, in an amendment contained in P.L. 104-99 (signed January 26, 1996), it amended the designated date as specified in the NVRA from March 11, 1993, to August 4, 1994.

Mississippi passed legislation giving state and local officials the authority to implement the NVRA, but only for federal elections. The state legislature established a dual registration system, providing that citizens who wished to cast a ballot in state and local elections had to register separately in accordance with prior registration law. On April 20, 1995, four citizens (later joined by the U.S. Department of Justice) sued over the dual registration requirements, charging that they violated the Voting Rights Act of 1965, as amended. On March 31, 1997, the Supreme Court ruled unanimously that Mississippi had violated the pre-clearance provisions of the Voting Rights Act when it chose to establish a dual voter registration system by applying the provisions of the NVRA solely to elections for federal office without first submitting the electoral changes for Justice Department approval. Mississippi had argued that, as it made no changes to state law, it did not need to seek pre -clearance for the new system, having already received clearance for its implementation plan of the NVRA provisions. As a result of the decision, Mississippi was required to submit its current dual registration system for approval by the Justice Department.[86] On October 5, 1998, a three-judge federal panel ordered Mississippi to allow all persons who registered under the NVRA provisions to vote in state and local elections until Mississippi enacted a law implementing the NVRA that was pre-cleared by the Justice Department. Subsequently (in 2000), Mississippi laws were brought into compliance.

After the first two years (1995-1996) of implementation, litigation, and an election, state and local officials appeared to come to terms with the NVRA. However, proposals were suggested to amend the NVRA to make it easier to administer and prevent election fraud. Some proposals suggested would (1) require a Social Security number on voter registration applications; (2) change the citizenship attestation to a question ["Are you a citizen?" YES NO] where applicants would have to say yes to be eligible to register; (3) eliminate the NVRA-mandated second mailings to persons already identified by the Postal Service as having moved; and (4) enact legislation to help reduce the costs of NVRA-mandated mailings.[87] Election officials formed a task force, the Joint Election Officials Liaison Committee (JEOLC) to negotiate and lobby for various changes in the law, as well as to work with the U.S. Postal Service to devise procedures that would make it easier for election offices to comply with some provisions of the NVRA. The JEOLC was composed of representatives from the International Association of Clerks, Recorders, Election Officials, and Treasurers (IACREOT), the National Association of County Recorders and Clerks (NACRC), the National Association of State Election Directors (NASED), and the Election Center.

A survey conducted by the National Association of Secretaries of State (NASS) of 43 states covered by the NVRA indicated that gains in voter registration had occurred in every state. Of the 43 states, 41 reported drivers' license bureaus effective in registering voters, and 35 indicated that other agencies also proved effective. More than half of the states indicated that their biggest problem was transmittal difficulties involving untimely, incomplete, unsigned, and illegible registration forms. About half thought that the NVRA restrictions on removing voters from the rolls contributed significantly to the greater number of registrants. However, other states applauded the NVRA for helping them maintain accurate registration lists.[88]

The Response of the Citizenry

Figure 1, below, based in large part on the most recent NVRA Report, displays voter registration[89] as a percentage of the voting-age population (VAP),[90] as a percentage of the citizen voting age population (CVAP),[91] and as a percentage of McDonald's voting eligible population (VEP)[92] in those states covered by the NVRA (44 states and the District of Columbia) for the period 1992-2012. Comparing only the differences in presidential election years, (depending on which measure one chooses) voter registration increased (7.9%—VAP, 11.4%—CVAP, or 10.6%—VEP) almost 8-11 percentage points between the pre-NVRA, 1992 presidential election and the 2012 presidential election.[93] The bulk of the change appears to have come immediately following the implementation of the NVRA.

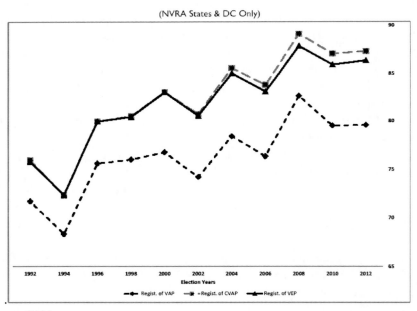

Source: ****

Notes: VAP, voting age population; CVAP, citizen voting age population; VEP, McDonalds's voting eligible population. Note that the percentage scale runs from 65% to 90%. This was done so that the distinction between the CVAP figures and the VEP figures could be shown.

Figure 1. Percentage of Voter Registration: 1992-2012.

As noted earlier, many proponents appeared to believe that the NVRA would not only increase voter registration but would also increase voter participation. Comparing post-NVRA voter turnout to the 1992 presidential election voter turnout might be somewhat misleading, as that election included a popular third-party candidate. **Figure 2** displays voter turnout for the NVRA covered states (as a % of the VAP, as a % of the CVAP and as a % of McDonald's VEP) in presidential elections since 1980.[94] In other words, voter turnout for presidential elections in the NVRA covered states has fluctuated between a low of less than 47.6% in 1996 to a high of over 56% in 2008. With the low and high turnout coming in the post-NVRA period, it is not clear whether NVRA has had an impact on voter turnout in presidential elections. On the one hand, there has been a steady increase (except for a slight drop in 2012) in voter turnout in presidential elections since 1996, the first post-NVRA presidential election year, of about 10 percentage points. On the other hand, only the 2008 election turnout exceeds the 1992, pre-NVRA presidential election turnout results. Similarly, voter turnout for these same states in non-presidential election years has been the following: 1982—40.1%, 1986—36.1%, 1990—36.0%, 1994—38.0%, 1998—34.6%, 2002 —35.7%, 2006—36.5%, and 2010—37.2%.[95] Mid-term elections have not shown much fluctuation since 1986. All-in -all, while the NVRA has been in effect for 18 years, there appears to be mixed evidence about the impact of the NVRA on increasing voter turnout. Of course, one could always argue that voter turnout might have been much worse without the NVRA, a rather difficult hypothesis to prove or disprove.

THE CONGRESSIONAL RESPONSE POST-NVRA[96]

The NVRA was not supported by most Republicans in the 103rd Congress, and a similar bill had been vetoed by President Bush in 1992. With the ascendancy of the Republican Party in the 104th Congress, and given the criticism of the NVRA as an "unfunded mandate" of the federal government by several prominent Republican governors from large states,[97] attempts to repeal or modify the NVRA appeared certain. However, while the Republican Party controlled both the House and Senate, its control in the Senate would not have prevented Democratic Senators from mounting a filibuster against proposals to change the NVRA. Further, with the White House in the hands of a Democrat (President Clinton) who supported the NVRA, any changes in the NVRA that were not bipartisan would almost certainly have been vetoed.

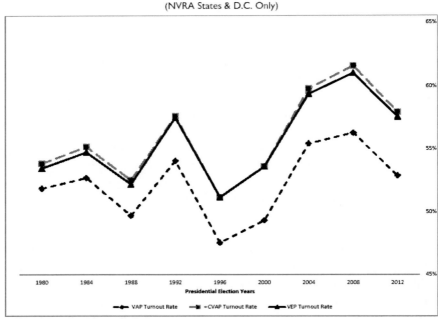

(NVRA States & D.C. Only)

Source: Table A-1, Table A-2.
Notes: VAP, voting age population; CVAP, citizen voting age population; VEP, McDonalds's voting eligible population. Note that the percentage scale runs from 45% to 65%. This was done so that the distinction between the CVAP figures and the VEP figures could be shown.

Figure 2. Percentage Voter Turnout, Presidential Elections: 1980-2012.

The 112th Congress saw the introduction of bills aimed at requiring states to establish same-day or election-day voter registration in all federal elections (H.R. 108, H.R. 3317, H.R. 3163, H.R. 5799/S. 3608); be able to update voter registration records at the polling place on election day (H.R. 3163); allow for Internet voter registration and use of the Internet to update statewide voter registration records (H.R. 5799/S. 3608, H.R. 6632); and, provide for the establishment of an automatic registration system based on information taken directly from state and federal agency database systems (H.R. 5799/S. 3608). In addition, legislation was proposed to require each voter registration agency (as defined under NVRA) within a state to insure that every registered voter, without charge, was issued a voter ID card if such voter ID was required by state law as a condition for voting in a federal election (H.R. 4126). Legislation also was proposed that would prevent any interference with voter registration (H.R. 5799/S. 3608), require the EAC to develop best practices for states to prevent such interference (H.R. 5799/S. 3608), and provide major penalties for promoting voter registration fraud (H.R. 6593/S. 168). Additionally, one bill, the Voter Empowerment Act of 2012 (H.R. 5799/S. 3608), provided that states must accept voter registration applications from otherwise qualified citizens 16 years of age and older, but the states were not required to make any changes in the age requirement for voting in state law. The same legislation specified that by 90 days after the end of every year, states must submit to the EAC specified statewide voter registration statistical information. It extended NVRA provisions and other provisions specific to the act to the District of Columbia, Puerto Rico, the U.S. Virgin Islands, Guam, and America Samoa. The Voter Empowerment Act of 2012 also established a pilot program to allow persons with disabilities to register (and to vote) from their residencies.

Other proposed legislation in the 112th Congress, among other things, provided for funding to states to explore appropriate technological changes to simplify the voter registration process within a state (H.R. 6590/S. 3635); required the Secretary of the Department of Veterans Affairs to specify local facilities within the Department as voter registration agencies as defined under NVRA (S. 1264); and designated a "National Month of Voter Registration (H.Res. 758/ S.Res. 572).

Thus far in the 113th Congress, much of the proposed legislation introduced duplicates legislative proposals introduced in the 112th Congress. This is true of the Voter Empowerment Act of 2013 (H.R. 12/S. 123 [H.R. 5799/S. 3608 in the 112th]), the Fair, Accurate, Secure, and Timely Voting Act or FAST Voting Act (H.R. 97/S. 85 [H.R. 6590/S. 3635 in the 112th]), the Same Day Registration Act of 2013 (H.R. 280/S. 532 [H.R. 3317 in the 112th]), the Value Our Time Elections or VOTE Act (H.R. 289 [H.R. 6632 in the 112th with a different title]), the Voter Fraud Prevention Act (H.R. 1280 [H.R. 6593/S. 168 in the 112th]), and the Voter Registration Efficiency Act (H.R. 2115 [H.R. 6386 in the 112th with a slightly different title]).

On June 4, 2013, the House Committee on House Administration held a hearing on the Voter Registration Efficiency Act (H.R. 2115). The bill is intended to reduce the number of voters registered in multiple states, among other things. The bill would amend the National Voter Registration Act of 1993 to require individuals registering to vote in a state to indicate if the state will be the individual's residence for the purpose of voting and for other purposes. The proposal is similar to an Arizona program, Interstate Cross - Check, in existence since 2009, matching records from 21 cooperating states.

According to Arizona Secretary of State Ken Bennett, in 2012, the cross-check located 45,000 duplicate voter registration records in Arizona from the other states.[98]

New legislative proposals in the 113th Congress direct the EAC to conduct a pilot program to provide funds to local educational agencies to instruct high school seniors about the voter registration process, the Students Voicing Opinions in Today's Elections (VOTE) Act (H.R. 653), applies directly all NVRA provisions to Puerto Rico, American Samoa, the Commonwealth of the Northern Mariana Islands, Guam, and the U.S. Virgin Islands (H.R. 1018), amends the NVRA to permit states to require documentary evidence to prove citizenship (H.R. 2409), and calls on the Congress to strengthen the "Nation's electoral system by ensuring clean and fair elections" (S. 9).

CONCLUSION

The National Voter Registration Act of 1993 has been the law of the land for over 20 years and has been in effect for 18 years. The courts have resolved many of the initial issues. A review of the FEC/EAC reports appears to indicate that the states have come to terms with the provisions, despite the fact that state election officials continue to advocate that the federal government should provide funding for the implementation of aspects of the act.

There may still be some problems with implementation at the local levels and with the training of nonelection officials who are responsible under the NVRA for providing voter registration services. As noted above, some opponents would like to curtail parts of the NVRA; proponents, however, do not think the NVRA has gone far enough. Some are calling for voter registration reform that would include what has been called "universal voter registration," where the government is responsible for registering all citizens to vote unlike the system used in the United States that relies on individuals to register themselves.[99] Others have suggested minor changes in NVRA, like making it "opt-out" instead of "opt-in" (i.e., automatic registration when an applicant receives a driver's license or benefits at designated state voter registration agencies, unless specifically deciding to "opt-out"), but with more enforcement of the provisions that are currently in place.[100] How and whether the Congress decides to respond to these calls for reform remains to be seen.

Table A-1. Percentage Voter Registration: 1992-2012
(NVRA States and DC only)

	Year	Voting Age Population (VAP)[a]	Total Reported Registration[a]	Percent Total Registration of VAP	Citizen Voting Age Population (CVAP)[b]	Percent Total Registration of CVAP	Voting Eligible Population (VEP)[b,c]	Percent Total Registration of VEP
National Summary for States Covered by NVRA (45 States)	2012	228,473,225	181,793,063	79.57	208,204,942	87.31	210,535,549	86.35
	2010	223,078,025	177,346,464	79.50	203,702,888	87.06	206,422,219	85.91
	2008	215,260,000	177,825,238	82.61	199,549,000	89.11	202,410,902	87.85
	2006	214,537,000	163,713,303	76.31	195,414,849	83.78	197,077,895	83.07
	2004	209,417,000	164,124,163	78.37	191,821,219	85.56	193,111,232	84.99
	2002	204,415,000	151,646,523	74.19	187,900,903	80.71	188,257,311	80.55
	2000	199,458,000	153,017,839	76.72	184,311,072	83.02	184,375,887	82.99
	1998	191,299,000	145,328,223	75.97	180,532,682	80.50	180,691,782	80.43
	1996	186,999,000	141,327,487	75.58	176,742,136	79.96	176,762,669	79.95
	1994	183,443,000	125,331,513	68.32	173,373,530	72.29	173,257,216	72.34
	1992	180,203,000	129,156,319	71.67	170,194,845	75.89	170,513,096	75.75
National Summary for States Not Covered by NVRA (ID, MN,	2012	11,712,727	9,934,459	84.82	11,288,706	88.00	11,390,271	87.22
	2010	11,486,046	9,458,748	82.35	11,091,440	85.28	10,988,813	86.08
	2008	11,315,000	10,059,488	88.90	10,927,000	92.06	10,902,606	92.27
	2006	11,127,000	9,029,403	81.15	10,736,724	84.10	10,565,699	85.46
	2004	10,963,000	9,534,261	86.97	10,528,352	90.56	10,372,224	91.92
	2002	10,660,000	8,994,452	84.38	10,303,908	87.29	10,124,629	88.84

Table A-1. (Continued)

	Year	Voting Age Population (VAP)[a]	Total Reported Registration[a]	Percent Total Registration of VAP	Citizen Voting Age Population (CVAP)[b]	Percent Total Registration of CVAP	Voting Eligible Population (VEP)[b,c]	Percent Total Registration of VEP
NH, ND, WI, WY	2000	10,369,000	9,481,940	91.45	10,091,787	93.96	9,955,549	95.24
	1998	9,971,000	8,677,330	87.03	9,869,769	87.92	9,727,789	89.20
	1996	9,790,000	9,063,714	92.58	9,692,065	93.52	9,584,375	94.57
	1994	9,567,000	8,645,722	90.37	9,462,243	91.37	9,366,132	92.31
	1992	9,326,000	8,782,267	94.17	9,226,214	95.19	9,142,427	96.06

Source: *NVRA Report 2011-2012*, Table 1a. Registration History, p. 14-31; United States Election Project, Voter Turnout, Google Doc spreadsheet for the full general election series from 1980-2012, http://elections.gmu.edu/voter_turnout.htm.

Notes:

a *NVRA Report 2011-2012*, Table 1a. Registration History, p. 14-31. The percentages are based on the figures in the column labeled "Reported Registration." Empty cells were completed by values from an earlier CRS Report, CRS Report 96-932, Voter Registration and Turnout: 1948-1994, by Royce Crocker (archived; available from the author). The table was then recomputed by the author based only on the 44 states and the District of Columbia covered by the NVRA.

b For the CVAP values for 2008, 2010, and 2012, see *NVRA Report 2011-2012*, Table 1a. Registration History, p. 14-31. For all other years, the values were derived from Professor Michael McDonald's percentages shown for non-citizen population from his spreadsheet for the full general election series from 1980-2012, see United States Election Project, Voter Turnout, Google Doc spreadsheet for the full general election series from 1980-2012, http://elections.gmu.edu/ voter_turnout.htm.

c For all years, the values were taken from Professor Michael McDonald's spreadsheet for the full general election series from 1980-2012, see United States Election Project, Voter Turnout, Google Doc spreadsheet for the full general election series from 1980-2012, http://elections.gmu.edu/voter_turnout.htm.

Table A-2. Voter Turnout: 1980-2012

	Year	VAP Turnout Rate	CVAP Turnout Rate	VEP Turnout Rate	Voting Age Population (VAP)	Citizen Voting Age Population (CVAP)	Voting-Eligible Population (VEP)	Vote for Highest Office
National Summary for States Covered by NVRA (45 States)	2012	52.9%	57.9%	57.5%	229,174,682	209,113,911	210,535,549	121,129,101
	2010	37.2%	40.8%	40.4%	224,478,172	204,550,501	206,422,219	83,484,726
	2008	56.2%	61.6%	61.0%	219,518,743	200,516,198	202,410,902	123,473,664
	2006	36.5%	40.0%	39.7%	214,365,179	195,414,849	197,077,895	78,184,498
	2004	55.4%	59.8%	59.4%	209,460,979	191,821,219	193,111,232	114,637,209
	2002	35.7%	38.9%	38.8%	204,827,709	187,900,903	188,257,311	73,076,854
	2000	49.3%	53.6%	53.6%	200,226,666	184,311,072	184,375,887	98,765,544
	1998	34.6%	37.4%	37.4%	195,172,053	180,532,682	180,691,782	67,595,964
	1996	47.6%	51.2%	51.1%	190,086,054	176,742,136	176,762,669	90,407,610
	1994	38.0%	40.7%	40.8%	185,591,574	173,373,530	173,257,216	70,603,818
	1992	54.0%	57.6%	57.5%	181,379,013	170,194,845	170,513,096	97,997,258
	1990	36.0%	38.2%	38.0%	176,990,353	166,845,637	167,671,505	63,663,174
	1988	49.7%	52.5%	52.2%	172,939,268	163,757,422	164,752,775	85,972,439
	1986	36.1%	37.9%	37.7%	169,072,114	160,814,374	161,713,342	60,956,054
	1984	52.7%	55.1%	54.7%	165,248,409	157,868,399	159,107,561	87,058,555
	1982[a]	40.1%	41.9%	41.6%	157,417,883	150,933,980	151,993,008	63,190,427
	1980	51.8%	53.8%	53.4%	156,032,668	150,310,795	151,347,591	80,890,341
National Summary for States Not Covered by NVRA	2012	67.6%	70.2%	69.7%	11,752,275	11,318,344	11,390,271	7,943,246
	2010	48.6%	50.4%	51.1%	11,544,817	11,132,348	10,988,813	5,614,750
	2008	69.0%	71.4%	71.8%	11,353,287	10,969,924	10,902,606	7,831,067
	2006	50.6%	52.4%	53.3%	11,120,220	10,736,724	10,565,699	5,631,094

Table A-2. (Continued)

	Year	VAP Turnout Rate	CVAP Turnout Rate	VEP Turnout Rate	Voting Age Population (VAP)	Citizen Voting Age Population (CVAP)	Voting-Eligible Population (VEP)	Vote for Highest Office
(ID, MN, NH, ND, WI, WY	2004	55.4%	72.7%	73.8%	10,875,040	10,528,352	10,372,224	7,657,769
	2002	49.9%	51.5%	52.4%	10,633,840	10,303,908	10,124,629	5,305,089
	2000	63.6%	65.5%	66.4%	10,396,742	10,091,787	9,955,549	6,609,942
	1998	48.7%	50.1%	50.8%	10,141,129	9,869,769	9,727,789	4,941,036
	1996	59.0%	60.4%	61.1%	9,929,863	9,692,065	9,584,375	5,855,325
	1994	46.6%	47.6%	48.1%	9,666,776	9,462,243	9,366,132	4,502,042
	1992	68.2%	69.5%	70.1%	9,398,910	9,226,214	9,142,427	6,407,897
	1990	45.8%	46.5%	46.8%	9,168,488	9,025,413	8,957,755	4,196,015
	1988	62.4%	63.3%	63.7%	9,016,216	8,888,464	8,826,505	5,622,252
	1986	45.6%	46.2%	46.5%	8,850,216	8,732,720	8,682,688	4,035,074
	1984	64.0%	64.8%	65.1%	8,746,201	8,637,884	8,594,343	5,594,125
	1982[a]	51.4%	52.0%	52.2%	8,609,751	8,510,680	8,473,911	4,425,149
	1980	66.9%	67.6%	67.9%	8,412,807	8,323,262	8,287,510	5,624,880

Source: United States Election Project, Voter Turnout, Google Doc spreadsheet for the full general election series from 1980-2012, http://elections.gmu.edu/ voter_turnout.htm.
[a] Excludes election results for the state of Louisiana.

APPENDIX B. POST-NVRA VOTER REGISTRATION LEGISLATIVE HISTORY, 104TH TO 111TH CONGRESSES

In the 105th Congress, as in the 104th, bills were introduced to repeal the NVRA (H.R. 345), to make the provisions voluntary (H.R. 2115), and to modify the provisions in some fashion. The modifications proposed consisted of the following: (1) requiring citizens to produce a Social Security number in order to register to vote (H.R. 224, H.R. 2076, and S. 1561); (2) requiring proof of citizenship in order to register to vote (H.R. 1139, H.R. 2076, and S. 1561); (3) allowing states to require photographic identification in order to cast a ballot (H.R. 1139 and S. 1561); (4) repealing the mail voter registration provisions of NVRA (H.R. 2076 and S. 1561); (5) changing purge rules in the NVRA to make it easier and less expensive for states to purge their voter registration rolls of ineligible persons (H.R. 2076, H.R. 3485, and S. 1561); and, (6) making optional for the states the requirement to allow registrants who change their address to vote at the polling place for their old address, the "failsafe voting" provision (H.R. 2076 and S. 1561).

In addition, Representative Horn introduced legislation that would have required the Immigration and Naturalization Service (INS) and the Social Security Administration, at the request of federal, state, or local election officials, to provide information on the citizenship status of persons attempting to register to vote (H.R. 1428).

The House Oversight Committee (renamed the Committee on House Administration in the 106th Congress) held hearings on H.R. 224, H.R. 1139, H.R. 1428, and H.R. 2076 on November 6, 1997. On February 12, 1998, H.R. 1428 was brought up for a vote under suspension of the rules in the House of Representatives, a procedure that requires a two-thirds majority to pass, and was defeated (vote: 210-200).

On March 18, 1998, Representative Thomas, then chairman of the Committee on House Oversight, introduced legislation (H.R. 3485) that, in part, would have established a pilot project in five states (California, New York, Texas, Florida, and Illinois) of the program proposed in H.R. 1428. H.R. 3485 was reported out of the Committee on House Oversight on March 23, 1998 (H.Rept. 105-457). On March 30, 1998, H.R. 3581, a revision of H.R. 3485, was introduced and brought up for a vote in the House, under suspended rules, and was defeated (vote: 74-337).

On May 6, 1998, the House passed (414-4) the Higher Education Amendments of 1998, H.R. 6, which contained an amendment offered by

Representative Clayton (H. Amdt. 583), requiring institutions of higher learning to distribute the NVRA mail voter registration application form to each student during enrollment, unless the student, in writing, declined such a form. The Senate version of H.R. 6 passed without this provision. In conference, the amendment was modified to require institutions in states covered by the NVRA to make "a good faith effort to distribute a mail voter registration form ... to each student enrolled in a degree or certified program." In addition, the revised language required the institutions to request voter registration forms from the state 120 days prior to the deadline for registering to vote, but it allowed an institution to implement its own program without interference from state officials. The conference report (H.Rept. 105-750) passed the House by voice vote September 28 and passed the Senate (vote: 96-0) September 29. The legislation was signed by President Clinton (P.L. 105-244) October 7, 1998.

As the 106th Congress began, two voter registration related bills were introduced in the House. On January 6, 1999, Representative Stump, as he did in the 105th Congress, introduced a bill (H.R. 38) to repeal the NVRA. On the same day, Representative McCollum introduced H.R. 180, a duplicate of the bill he introduced in the 105th Congress (H.R. 224). In May, Senator Warner introduced legislation to deal with campaign finance reform (S. 1107). S. 1107, essentially a duplicate of S. 1561, introduced in the 105th Congress, see above). This bill amended parts of the NVRA by (1) repealing the mail voter registration requirements, (2) requiring states to obtain an applicant's Social Security number when attempting to register to vote, (3) requiring applicant's registering at a state motor vehicle office to submit proof of citizenship, (4) allowing states to purge names from voter registration lists because the registrants had failed to vote for period of time after the registrant was notified, and (5) repealing the limited provisional voting provisions of the NVRA. In September, 1999, Representative Luther introduced legislation to amend the NVRA by requiring states to provide citizens the right to register at the polling place on election-day (H.R. 2864). There was no action on any of these bills in the 106th Congress.

In reaction to the events of the 2000 Presidential election, a number of bills were introduced in the 107th Congress to reform the election administration process. While some of these bills focused solely on voter registration (H.R. 128, H.R. 189, H.R. 829, H.R. 2687, S. 2226), much of the effort was focused on a more comprehensive response. The efforts culminated in the passage of the Help America Vote Act of 2002 (HAVA) (P.L. 107-252). HAVA addressed voter registration in four areas:

(1) it created the Election Assistance Commission (EAC) and transferred FEC's responsibilities with respect to NVRA to EAC (§201; §202; §209; §803), specifically with respect to the development and maintenance of the federal mail voter registration form (§303(b)(4)) and the biennial reports on the impact of the NVRA;

(2) it specified that each state "shall implement, in a uniform and nondiscriminatory manner, a single, uniform, official, centralized, interactive computerized statewide voter registration list defined, maintained, and administered at the State level that contains the name and registration information of every legally registered voter in the State and assigns a unique identifier to each legally registered voter in the State" (§303(a)(1)(A)) and "perform list maintenance with respect to the computerized list on a regular basis" in accordance with the provisions of NVRA (§303(a)(2));

(3) it required the use of the driver's license number or the last four digits of the social security number of the applicant on all voter registration applications (§303(a)(5)(A)), as well as requiring that the Social Security Administration develop relationships with the departments of motor vehicles in each state to assist in list verification (§303(a)(5)(B); and,

(4) it expanded the "fail safe voting" provisions of NVRA to provisional voting (§303(a)(5)(A)-(B)).

In the 108th Congress, legislation was introduced to repeal NVRA (H.R. 2139), to require proof of citizenship to register to vote (H.R. 4174, H.R. 4530), to standardize the treatment of ex-felons with respect to their right to register to vote (H.R. 1433, H.R. 4758), to require states "to provide notice and an opportunity for review prior to removing any individual from the official list of eligible voters by reason of criminal conviction or mental incapacity" (H.R. 4250), to require same-day or election-day voter registration (H.R. 1510, H.R. 3153), and to allow pre-registration to individuals to register to vote prior to meeting the age requirement (H.R. 4972). None of the bills reached beyond the committee assignment.

In the 109th Congress, legislation was introduced to require states to institute same-day or election-day voter registration (H.R. 496, H.R. 533, H.R. 939, H.R. 3557, S. 17. S. 450), to require proof of citizenship when registering (H.R. 4989), to require a photo-identification when registering to vote (H.R. 2250), to allow removal from registration lists for failure to vote (H.R. 2778), to prohibit removal from voter registration lists due to correctable errors and removal for felony conviction or death unless the comparison database meet standards set by the Director of the National Institute of Standards and Technology (H.R. 3094), to delay the implementation of the state voter registration database requirement in HAVA for four years (H.R. 3163), to require states to keep the name and addresses of victims of domestic violence that appeared on state voter registration databases confidential (H.R. 4462), and to require states to produce durable voter registration cards (H.R. 4989). One other bill, S. 414, had several goals. It would have required the use of the Social Security number in registering voters, required that all states synchronize all state voter registration databases, eliminated third party voter registration, modified conditions for removal of names from voter registration databases, and clarified procedures for first-time registrants. None of the bills reached the floor of the House or the Senate.

The legislative activity in the 110th Congress, in many ways, reproduced that in the 109th. Same-day or election-day voter registration was introduced in a variety of bills (H.R. 2457, H.R. 5628, H.R. 1381, H.R. 5946, S. 730, S. 804, S. 2959). Three bills contained provisions aimed at requiring notice before any names could be removed from voter registration lists (H.R. 7244, S. 730, S. 804). Legislation also was introduced to control by whom and how voter registration forms were distributed (H.R. 301), to require the acceptance of any type of voter registration form sent by overseas military or civilians (S. 3073), to require the acceptance of a newly created official federal voter registration and ballot application from overseas citizens (H.R. 4237), to make institutions of higher education state voter registration agencies as specified in NVRA (S. 3390, H.R. 6704), to require the addition of a statement on voter registration application forms that stated that any alien who used the form to register was deportable under the Immigration and Nationality Act (H.R. 5695), to prohibit states from not accepting voter registration forms from third parties (S. 1487), to require photographic identification to register to vote (H.R. 879), to promote pre-registration for students under 18 (S. 3100), and to have the EAC study Internet voter registration (S. 730, S. 804). The only legislation that passed the House, however, was a bill that required the Department of Veterans Affairs to designate all of its public facilities as state voter registration agencies as defined under NVRA (H.R. 6625). This bill was not acted upon in the Senate.

The 111th Congress saw the introduction of bills aimed at requiring states to establish same-day voter registration or election-day registration (H.R. 105, H.R. 3957, S. 1986). Bills were introduced containing provisions aimed at requiring notice before names could be removed from statewide voter registration databases (H.R. 105, H.R. 3416, H.R. 3835). Also, bills were introduced requiring or promoting states to adopt on-line or Internet voter registration procedures (H.R. 105, H.R. 1719, H.R. 4449, S. 3301). Bills were also introduced to add to the list of official voter registration agencies, as designated in NVRA, by adding universities (H.R. 1729, S. 1125), or by adding Department of Veterans Administration facilities (S. 1556), or by designating an office on each military installation as a voter registration agency (H.R. 3274, S. 1265). Other bills were introduced to regulate or minimize challenges to voter registration status on election-day at the polling place (H.R. 103, H.R. 105). One bill, which concerned various aspects of the election process, required states and the EAC to replace specific questions on voter registration application forms about either age or citizenship or both with a signed affidavit on the form (H.R. 105). Another bill (H.R. 3489) would have amended HAVA to prevent any challenge to eligibility to register to vote due to foreclosure proceedings being brought against the voter. Another proposal (S. 1103) would establish standards for the distribution of voter registration forms, and would require organizations to register with the state prior to distributing such forms.

While a few of the above proposed bills were discussed in hearings, none came to the floor or were voted on by either chamber. However, on October 28, 2009, the President signed into law the Military and Overseas Vote Empowerment (MOVE) Act (S. 1415, P.L. 111-84, 123 Stat. 2190 (2009)), which, in part amended the Uniform and Overseas Citizens Absentee Voting Act (UOCAVA). Signed into law as part of the National Defense Authorization Act of 2009 (H.R. 2647/S. 1390, §575, P.L. 111-84, 123 Stat. 2318, [42 U.S.C.A. §1971]), the MOVE Act made changes to certain absentee voting laws and procedures that apply to military and overseas voters. With respect to changes in voter registration procedures, the act established procedures for absent uniform service voters and overseas voters to request and for states to send voter registration applications and absentee ballot applications by mail and electronically (P.L. 111 -84, §577(a), [42 U.S.C.A. §1973ff-1]). The act also prohibited refusal to accept voter registration applications, absentee ballot applications, marked absentee ballots and federal write-in absentee ballots for failure to meet certain requirements ("notarization requirements," "restrictions on paper type, including weight and size," and "restrictions on envelope type, including weight and size")(P.L. 111-84, §582(a)-(c), [42 U.S.C.A. §1973ff-1(i), §1973ff-2(f)]).

In addition, the act amends Chapter 80, of Title 10, United States Code, pertaining to the military, by requiring that "the Secretaries of the military departments shall designate offices on installations under their jurisdiction to provide absent uniformed service voters, ..."

> "(1) Information on voter registration procedures and absentee ballot procedures...."
>
> "(2) Information and assistance, if requested, including access to the Internet where practicable, to register to vote in an election for federal office, ..." (P.L. 111-84 §583(b), 10 U.S.C.A. §1566a(a)-(d)).

Also, the Secretaries of the military departments may designate these voter assistance offices as "voter registration agencies" on military installations under Section 7(a)(2) of the NVRA of 1993 (P.L. 103-31.[42 U.S.C. 1973gg-5(a)(2)]) (P.L. 111-84, §583(b), [10 U.S.C.A. §1566(e)]). In other words, the act requires that all installations of the military have voter assistance offices to help absent uniformed service voters with voter registration applications as well as with assistance acquiring absentee ballots. At the discretion of the Secretaries of each military department, these offices may be designated as voter registration agencies. If so designated, these offices would be authorized to accept voter registration applications and transmit to the appropriate state election officials within the specified time frame indicated in the NVRA. However, the Secretary of Defense has the authority to changes these procedures through regulations (P.L. 111-84, §583(b), [10 U.S.C.A. §1566A(f)]).

In the process leading up to the passage of the MOVE Act, several bills were also introduced to modify UOCAVA that would have modified voter registration practices as well (H.R. 1659, H.R. 1739, H.R. 2823, H.R. 3416, H.R. 3473). The bills either never reached the floor or provisions were incorporated into the MOVE Act.

End Notes

[1] For a detailed discussion, see CRS's Legal Sidebar, "Supreme Court Rules: Arizona Law Requiring Proof of Citizenship for Voter Registration Preempted by Federal Law," by Paige Whitaker, http://www.crs.gov/LegalSidebar/ details.aspx?ID=558&Source=ibc.

[2] CRS Report RS20764, *The Uniformed and Overseas Citizens Absentee Voting Act: Overview and Issues*, by Kevin J. Coleman.

[3] U.S. Congress, House Committee on House Administration, *Voter Registration*, hearings on H.R. 15, H.R. 17 and H.R. 87, 101st Cong., 1st sess., March 21, 1989 (Washington: GPO, 1989).

[4] U.S. Congress, Senate Committee on Rules and Administration, *National Voter Registration Act of 1993*, report to accompany S. 460, 103rd Cong., 1st sess., S. Rept. 103-6, (Washington: GPO, 1993), p. 7.

[5] Ibid., p. 5

[6] Subsequently delegated to the Election Assistance Commission (EAC) when FEC functions were transferred because of HAVA in 2002 (P.L. 107-252, title VIII, §802(a), Oct. 29, 2002, 116 Stat. 1726., U.S.C. 42 §15532).

[7] These provisions were strengthened somewhat by HAVA, P.L. 107-252 (42 U.S.C., §15483 (2)(A)) by requiring that the new required statewide voter registration database be compared to other appropriate statewide databases.

[8] The provision about "failure to vote in two consecutive elections" was clarified in HAVA, P.L. 107-252 (42 U.S.C. §15483 (4)).

[9] Again, these functions were transferred to the EAC by HAVA, P.L. 107-252, see footnote 6.

[10] U.S. Congress, Senate Committee on Rules and Administration, *National Voter Registration Act of 1993*, report to accompany S. 460, 103rd Cong., 1st sess., S. Rept. 103-6, (Washington: GPO, 1993), p. 5.

[11] Ibid., pp. 51-52.

[12] For a different view of "decreasing voter turnout," see Michael P. McDonald and Samuel Popkin, "The Myth of the Vanishing Voter," *American Political Science Review*, vol. 94, no. 4 (2001), pp. 963-974.

[13] Sen. Mitch McConnell, "National Voter Registration Act of 1992," remarks in the Senate, daily edition, vol. 138, Sept. 21, 1992, p. S14206.

[14] Ibid., pp. 2-3. Also see U.S. Congress, House Committee on House Administration, *National Voter Registration Act of 1993*, report to accompany H.R. 2, 103rd Cong., 1st sess., H. Rept. 103-9 (Washington: GPO, 1993), pp. 2-5.

[15] S. Rept. 103-6, pp. 50-51.

[16] Ibid., p. 51. H. Rept. 103-9, p. 36.

[17] Sen. Mitch McConnell, "National Voter Registration Act of 1992," remarks in the Senate, daily edition, vol. 138, Sept. 21, 1992, p. S14206.

[18] Sen. Daniel K. Akaka, "National Voter Registration Act of 1993," remarks in the Senate, *Congressional Record*, vol. 139, Mar. 17, 1993, p. S3002.

[19] S. Rept. 103-6, p. 41.

[20] S. Rept. 103-6, pp. 2, 5.

[21] The Federal Election Commission, *The Impact of the National Voter Registration Act of 1993 on the Administration of Elections for Federal Office 1995-1996*, Washington, DC, June 30, 1997, p.14.

[22] Ibid., p. 14.

[23] Ibid., p. 15. These are the figures for the 1995-1996 period. Comparable figures given for the 2001-2002 period were 160,000,000, 20,000,000, 4,000,000, and 37,000,000, respectively. See, the *2001-2002 NVRA Report*, The Federal Election Commission, *The Impact of the National Voter Registration Act of 1993 on the Administration of Elections for Federal Office 2001-2002*, Washington, DC, June 30, 2003, p. 24.

[24] *NVRA Report 1995-1996*, p. 15.

[25] Lisa Gilbert, *Saving Dollars, Saving Democracy: Cost Savings for Local Election Officials through Voter Registration Modernization*, U.S. PIRG, May 2009, p. 3.

[26] Ibid., p. 3.

[27] Ibid., pp. 3-4, 20.

[28] Ibid., p.20.

[29] S. Rept. 103-6, pp. 52-57. H. Rept. 103-9, pp. 34-37.

[30] HAVA requires that language to this effect be included in the mail registration form developed by the Election Assistance Commission (EAC).(U.S.C. 42 §15483(b)(4)(A)(i)).

[31] S. Rept. 103-6, pp. 5, 11-13, 20-21, 37. H. Rept. 103-9, pp. 10-11, 14, 20-21.

[32] See also, Barry H. Weinberg, *The Resolution of Election Disputes: Legal Principles That Control Election Challenges, 2ⁿᵈ Edition* (Washington, DC: International Foundation for Electoral Systems, 2008), pp. 85-101.

[33] For a full discussion of the Help America Vote Act, see CRS Report RL32685, *Election Reform: The Help America Vote Act and Issues for Congress*, by Eric A. Fischer and Kevin J. Coleman.

[34] For a clear description of how the FEC determined its reporting requirements and, thus the reporting requirements of the states, see Federal Election Commission, *The Impact of the National Voter Registration Act of 1993 on the Administration of Elections for Federal Office 1995-1996*, Washington, DC, June 30, 1997, henceforth, *NVRA Report 1995-1996*.

[35] *NVRA Report 1995-1996*; Federal Election Commission, *The Impact of the National Voter Registration Act of 1993 on the Administration of Elections for Federal Office 1993-1994*, Washington, DC, June 30, 1995, henceforth known as *NVRA Report 1993-1994*; Federal Election Commission, *The Impact of the National Voter Registration Act of 1993 on the Administration of Elections for Federal Office 1997-1998*, Washington, DC, June 30, 1999, henceforth known as *NVRA Report 1997-1998*; Federal Election Commission, *The Impact of the National Voter Registration Act of 1993 on the Administration of Elections for Federal Office, 1999-2000*, Washington, DC, June 30, 2001, henceforth, known as *NVRA Report 1999-2000*; Federal Election Commission, *The Impact of the National Voter Registration Act of 1993 on the Administration of Elections for Federal Office 2001-2002*, Washington, DC, June 30, 2003, henceforth, known as *NVRA Report 2001-2002*; Elections Assistance Commission, *The Impact of the National Voter Registration Act of 1993 on the Administration of Elections for Federal Office 2003-2004*, Washington, DC, June 30, 2005, henceforth, known as *NVRA Report 2003-2004*; Elections Assistance Office, *The Impact of the National Voter Registration Act of 1993 on the Administration of Elections for Federal Office 2005-2006*, Washington, DC, June 30, 2007, henceforth known as *NVRA Report 2005-2006*; Elections Assistance Office, *The Impact of the National Voter Registration Act of 1993 on the Administration of Elections for Federal Office 2007-2008*, Washington, DC, June 30, 2009, henceforth known as *NVRA Report 2007-2008*; Elections Assistance Office, *The Impact of the National Voter Registration Act of 1993 on the Administration of Elections for Federal Office 2009-2010*, Washington, DC, June 30, 2011, henceforth known as NVRA Report 2009-2010; Elections Assistance Office, *The Impact of the National Voter Registration Act of 1993 on the Administration of Elections for Federal Office 2011-12*, Washington, DC, June 30, 2013, henceforth known as *NVRA Report 2011-2012*.

[36] *NVRA Report 1995-1996*, p. 1.

[37] *NVRA Report 1995-1996*, pp. 1-2.

[38] *NVRA Report 1995-1996*, pp. 2-3.

[39] *NVRA Report 1997-1998*, p. 1.

[40] *NVRA Report 1997-1998*, pp. 1-2.

[41] *NVRA Report 1999-2000*, p. 1.

[42] *NVRA Report 1999-2000*, pp. 1-2.

[43] *NVRA Report 1999-2000*, pp. 3-4.

[44] *NVRA Report 2001-2002*, p. 1.

[45] *NVRA Report 2001-2002*, pp. 1-2.

[46] *NVRA Report 2001-2002*, p. 14.

[47] See *NVRA Report 1995-1996*, pp. 37-43, *NVRA Report 1997-1998*, pp. 21-26, *NVRA Report 1999-2000*, pp. 29-35. Also, on May 4, 1995, in testimony before the Senate Subcommittee on Treasury, Postal Service, and General Government of the Senate Appropriations Committee, Postmaster General Marvin Runyon noted that the NVRA cost the agency $2.1 million dollars that year and described it as an "unfunded mandate" for the Postal Service. Under the NVRA, the Postal Service is required to provide the states with "third-class" rates, available to nonprofit organizations, for voter registration mailings. However, several states have complained that it is almost impossible to comply with certain provisions of the

NVRA relating to voter list maintenance because the Postal Service does not, under nonprofit mailing rates, normally return non-forwardable mailings to the sender. Non-forwardable mailings can be used as a first step in determining if a citizen has moved from an old address under the NVRA.

[48] *NVRA Report 1999-2000*, pp. 35-37.

[49] *NVRA Report 2001-2002*, p. 3.

[50] *NVRA Report 2003-2004*, p. 1-2, 9-12.

[51] *NVRA Report 2003-2004*, pp. 9-12.

[52] *NVRA Report 2003-2004*, pp. 13-14.

[53] *NVRA Report 2005-2006*, p. 1.

[54] *NVRA Report 2005-2006*, pp. 1-2.

[55] *NVRA Report 2005-2006*, pp. 13-14.

[56] *NVRA Report 2007-2008*, p. 29.

[57] *NVRA Report 2007-2008*, p. 1.

[58] *NVRA Report 2007-2008*, p. 1.

[59] *NVRA Report 2007-2008*, pp. 1-2.

[60] *NVRA Report 2007-2008*, p. 1.

[61] *NVRA Report 2007-2008*, p. 39.

[62] *NVRA Report 2007-2008*, pp. 8-9.

[63] *NVRA Report 2009-2010*, p. 29.

[64] *NVRA Report 2009-2010*, p. 1 and *NVRA Report 2005-2006*, p. 2.

[65] *NVRA Report 2009-2010*, p. 1.

[66] *NVRA Report 2009-2010*, p. 2.

[67] *NVRA Report 2009-2010*, p. 1.

[68] *NVRA Report 2009-2010*, Table 2a. Application Sources: Total Forms Received, pp. 38-39.

[69] *NVRA Report 2009-2010*, p. 9.

[70] *NVRA Report 2011-2012*, "Table 1a. Registration History," pp. 14-31. Figures were computed for the 44 states and the District of Columbia by the author.

[71] *NVRA Report 2011-2012*, p. 1.

[72] *NVRA Report 2011-2012*, p. 2.

[73] *NVRA Report 2011-2012*, p. 2.

[74] *NVRA Report 2011-2012*, p. 6.

[75] *NVRA Report 2011-2012*, "Table 2a. Application Sources: Total Forms Received," pp. 40-41.

[76] *NVRA Report 2011-2012*, "Table 2a. Application Sources: Total Forms Received," pp. 40-41.

[77] *NVRA Report 2011-2012*, pp. 9-10.

[78] *U.S. v. New York*, 3 F. Supp. 2d 298 (E.D. NY); *U.S v. New York*, 255 F. Supp. 2c 73 (E.D. NY); 2007 U.S. Dist. LEXIS 21722.

[79] 2006 U.S. Dist. LEXIS 45640.

[80] 2006 U.S. Dist. LEXIS 32499.

[81] Based on a LEXIS search covering the period, searching for the "National Voter Registration Act."

[82] Michael Slater, "Compliance with the NVRA: Not Optional," *The National Voter*, February 2008, pp. 11-12, http://www.lwv.org/AM/Template.cfm?Section=Home&Template=/ TaggedPage/TaggedPageDisplay.cfm&TPLID= 19&ContentID=10530.

[83] Applications received from state voter registration agencies in the 1995-1996 period constituted 11% of all applications received. The same was true in the 2003-2004 period and the 2005-2006 periods, see *NVRA Report, 1995-1996*, pp. 1-2; *NVRA Report 2003-2004*, pp. 9-12; *NVRA Report 2005-2006*, pp. 1-2. However, during the 2007-2008 period this percentage dropped to 6.3%, see *NVRA Report 2007-2008*, p. 39. For the 2009-2010 election cycle, this percentage dropped even further to 5.6%, see *NVRA Report 2009-2010*, p. 39. For the most recent election cycle, this figure is 6.3%, see *NVRA Report 2011-2012*, p. 41.

[84] See Jordy Yager, "Schumer Wants States Sued Over Voter Registration," http://thehill.com/ leading-the-news/schumer-wants-states-sued-over-voter-registration-2009-04-07.html. Also, see Sen. Schumer's website at http://schumer.senate.gov/new_website/record.cfm? id=311271. Also, Senator Charles Schumer, "Schumer Urges DOJ: Sue States That Flout Voter Registration Law," press release, April 7, 2009, http://schumer.senate.gov/new_ website/record.cfm?id=311271.

[85] See, "Project Vote Applauds Justice Department Enforcement of NVRA in Illinois," http://www.reuters.com/article/ pressRelease/idUS53510+20-Dec-2008+PRN20081220.

[86] *Young* et al. *v. Fordice* et al. 520 U.S. 273 (1997), see http://www.law.cornell.edu/supct/ html/95-2031.ZS.html.

[87] Richard G. Smolka, "Election Officials Liaison Group Advised of Legislative Opportunities, Postal Rate Increase," in *Election Administration Reports*, vol. 27 (Washington: Jan. 13, 1997), pp. 2-4; Richard G. Smolka, "JEOLC Hears Congressional Staff Outline Plans for Legislation," in *Election Administration Reports*, vol. 28 (Washington: Jan. 19, 1998), p. 5.

[88] Richard G. Smolka, "NASS Survey Identifies Gains and Some Problems with NVRA," in *Election Administration Reports*, vol. 27 (Washington: Feb. 13, 1997), pp. 1-3.

[89] *NVRA Report 2011-2012*, Table 1a. Registration History, p. 14-31. The percentages are based on the figures in the column labeled "Reported Registration." Empty cells were completed by values from CRS Report 96-932, *Voter Registration and Turnout: 1948-1994*, by Royce Crocker (archived; available from the author). The table was then recomputed by the author based only on the 44 states and the District of Columbia covered by the NVRA. See ****.

[90] *NVRA Report 2011-2012*, Table 1a. Registration History, p. 14-31.

[91] For the CVAP values for 2008, 2010, and 2012, see *NVRA Report 2011-2012*, Table 1a. Registration History, p. 14-31. For all other years, the values were derived from Professor Michael McDonald's percentages shown for the non-citizen population from his spreadsheet for the full general election series from 1980-2012, see United States Election Project, Voter Turnout, Google Doc spreadsheet for the full general election series from 1980-2012, http://elections.gmu.edu/voter_turnout.htm.

[92] For all years, the values were derived from Professor Michael McDonald's spreadsheet for the full general election series from 1980-2012, see United States Election Project, Voter Turnout, Google Doc spreadsheet for the full general election series from 1980-2012, http://elections.gmu.edu/voter_turnout.htm.

[93] See ****, below.

[94] Turnout figures come from Michael P. McDonald, United States Election Project—Voter Turnout, Excel Turnout Spreadsheet, "Turnout 1980-2012.xls," http://elections.gmu.edu/ voter_turnout.htm. The author computed turnout for the states covered by NVRA provisions from McDonald's spreadsheet. Turnout figures are based on 'vote totals for highest office." It should be noted that McDonald does not recommend using the voting-age population as the divisor for computing turnout, preferring his Voter Eligible Population measure. This is, without question a better measure, especially when making comparisons between states and countries. However, for historical consistency with the figures used by the FEC (EAC), this author chose to include figures based on the voting-age population, as well. See **Appendix A, Table A-2**.

[95] Ibid., see McDonald, United States Election Project—Voter Turnout, Excel Turnout Spreadsheet, "Turnout 1980 - 2012.xls," http://elections.gmu.edu/voter_turnout.htm. For the mid-term elections in these states, see **Appendix A, Table A-2**.

[96] For the legislative history of the 104th to 111th Congresses with respect to voter registration proposed legislation, see **Appendix B**.

[97] Alan Greenblat, "Court Rejects 'Motor Voter' Case, But the Battle Isn't Over," Congressional Quarterly, weekly report, vol. 54 (Washington: Jan. 27, 1996), p. 232.

[98] John T. Willis, "Committee on House Administration Holds Hearing on Voter Efficiency Act," *Election Administration Reports*, vol. 43, no. 12 (June 10, 2013), pp. 3-4.

[99] Wendy Weiser, Michael Waldman, and Renee Paradis, *Voter Registration Modernization*, Brennan Center for Justice, New York University School of Law, New York, NY, 2009, http://www.brennancenter.org/content/resource/universal_voter_registration_draft_summary/; FairVote, "Universal Voter Registration, http://www.fairvote.org/?page= 65; Progressive States Network, "Universal Voter Registration: A New Initiative to Increase Electoral Participation and Reduce Voter Suppression, http://www.progressivestates.org/node/22476.

[100] Common Cause, "Voter Registration," http://www.commoncause.org/site/pp.asp?c= dkLNK1MQIwG&b=4923169.

In: National Voter Registration Act   ISBN: 978-1-63117-829-0
Editor: Aaliyah Garner   © 2014 Nova Science Publishers, Inc.

Chapter 2

THE IMPACT OF THE NATIONAL VOTER REGISTRATION ACT OF 1993 ON THE ADMINISTRATION OF ELECTIONS FOR FEDERAL OFFICE 2011–2012[*]

U.S. Election Assistance Commission

EXECUTIVE SUMMARY

This report to the United States Congress addresses the impact of the National Voter Registration Act (NVRA) of 1993 on the administration of elections for Federal office for the 2012 election cycle, i.e., the two-year period following the November 2010 elections through the November 2012 presidential election.

The 2012 report is based on the results of a survey of all States, the District of Columbia, and three territories—American Samoa, Guam, and Puerto Rico—conducted by the Election Assistance Commission (EAC). The U.S. Virgin Islands did not respond to the 2012 survey.

As with past reports, the quality and completeness of responses from many States and territories varied significantly.

Six States and all territories are exempt from the provisions of the NVRA.[1] Other States did not collect voter registration data in a way that was

---

[*] This is an edited, reformatted and augmented version of a report to the 113th Congress, dated June 30, 2013.

compatible with a few of the survey questions. Jurisdictions in a few States faced challenges in collecting the data, hampering the States' abilities to provide complete data for all jurisdictions[2]

The survey shows that the number of registered voters increased during the 2012 election cycle. There were approximately 194.2 million total registered voters reported for the November 2012 presidential election, an increase of over 7.3 million registered voters from the 2010 elections. It is important to note that Puerto Rico did not hold Federal elections in 2010. As such, the 2.4 million reported registrations in Puerto Rico contribute to this overall increase in registration. The number of registered voters in 2012 represents an increase of approximately 3.7 million voters since the 2008 presidential election cycle.[3]

According to the responses to the survey and population estimates from the U.S. Census Bureau, 87.4% of American citizens of voting age (18 years or older) were registered to vote in the 2012 elections.

Five States reported a large increase in active registrants compared to the previous presidential election held in 2008, while five States reported a dramatic decrease. Since the previous presidential election, the District of Columbia, South Carolina, and Ohio reported an increase of over 10% in the number of active registrants, and Hawaii and Mississippi indicated an increase of over 20%; Michigan and Nebraska reported a decrease of over 10%, and New Mexico, New York, and South Dakota reported a decrease of over 20%.[4] Active registrants refers to all registered voters except those who have been sent, but who have not responded to a confirmation mailing sent in accordance with NVRA (42 U.S.C. 1973gg-6(d)) and have not since offered to vote.

Other highlights of the 2012 NVRA study include:

- States reported receiving over 62.5 million voter registration application forms. Use of mail, fax, or email to submit forms increased from the previous election cycle, with 23.3% of registration forms being delivered through these means. Another 16.4% of applications were submitted in person at elections or registrars offices, and 32.4% were submitted at motor vehicle agencies. Twenty-one States reported receiving voter registration applications over the Internet.
- Of the 62.5 million voter registration forms received, over 23.8 million of the applications were from new voters not previously registered in the local jurisdiction or who had not previously registered in any jurisdiction. There was a surge in new applications

during the 2012 election cycle, with 23.8 million new registrants, compared to the 2010 election cycle that had 14.4 million new registrants. However, this represents slightly fewer new registrants than in the 2008 presidential election when there were 24.7 million new registrants.

- Nearly 27.5 million of the registration forms that were submitted requested a change of name, address, or party of the registrant within the registrant's current jurisdiction.
- Nearly 439,000 voter registration applications were "pre-registrations" from people under the age of 18, who were registering under State laws that allow them to pre-register to vote before the age of 18 and vote upon turning 18 (or in a primary if they would be 18 by the general election). This number dramatically increased from the 2010 election cycle when approximately 168,000 pre-registrations were processed.
- States found invalid or otherwise rejected over 5.0 million applications, and nearly 3.7 million applications were duplicates of existing registrations. Altogether, 13.9% of registration applications were invalid or duplicates.
- States sent 17.5 million address confirmation notices to names on their registration rolls, as allowed by the NVRA. More States were able to provide the number of voters that were removed than the number of confirmation notices sent.
- States removed nearly 13.7 million voters from voter registration lists, for reasons including death, felony conviction, failure to respond to notices sent and vote in consecutive Federal elections, having moved from one jurisdiction to another, or at the voter's request.
- The survey collected information on Election Day Registration, in which voters can register and vote on the same day, either during early voting periods or on Election Day itself. Twenty States reported adding nearly 1.4 million new registrants to their voter lists on days during which voters could also cast their ballots. Same Day Registration accounted for approximately 30% of total applications received during the 2012 election cycle in Wisconsin and Wyoming, and more than 20% of total applications in Idaho, Maine, and Minnesota.

SECTION 1. ABOUT THE NVRA

Purposes and Requirements of the National Voter Registration Act

The primary objectives of the NVRA are:

- To establish procedures that will increase the number of eligible citizens who register to vote in elections for Federal office;
- To protect the integrity of the electoral process by ensuring that accurate and current voter registration rolls are maintained; and
- To enhance the participation of eligible citizens as voters in elections for Federal office [42 U.S.C. §1973gg].

The NVRA pursues these objectives by:

- Expanding the number of locations and opportunities whereby eligible citizens may apply to register to vote;
- Requiring voter registration file maintenance procedures that, in a uniform and nondiscriminatory manner, identify and remove the names of only those individuals who are no longer eligible to vote; and
- Providing registration requirements and procedures to ensure that an individual's right to vote prevails over current bureaucratic or legal technicalities.[5]

Expanding Opportunities to Register to Vote

Before enactment of the NVRA, the locations and opportunities for eligible citizens to register to vote in Federal elections varied widely throughout the States. Evidence from State experimentation with different registration policies suggested that expanding the number of locations and opportunities for voter registration resulted in increased registration for Federal elections.

To address this, the NVRA requires that individuals be given a voter registration application when applying for or renewing a driver's license, or when applying for (or receiving) services at certain other public offices.[6] The NVRA also requires States to accept registration by mail for Federal elections.

Voter Registration File Maintenance

The NVRA requires States to conduct a program to maintain the integrity of the electoral process by ensuring accurate and current voter registration rolls [42 U.S.C. §1973gg-6]. Such a program may not remove the name of a voter from the list of eligible voters due to a person's failure to vote. However, States are permitted to remove the names of eligible voters from the rolls at the request of the voter or as provided by State law for reason of mental incapacity or criminal conviction. In addition, States are required to conduct a general program that makes a reasonable effort to remove the names of ineligible voters from the official lists by reason of death or change of residence [42 U.S.C. §1973gg6]. The NVRA requires that any such program be "uniform, nondiscriminatory, and in compliance with the Voting Rights Act of 1965..." [42 U.S.C. §1973gg].

"Fail-Safe" Voting Procedures

Congress, in considering the NVRA, believed that registrants were sometimes denied the right to vote on Election Day, either because of some oversight on their part or because of a clerical error by an election official. Registrants who changed residence within a jurisdiction, for example, often mistakenly assumed they were still entitled to vote, only to discover on Election Day that their failure to re-register at their new address had disenfranchised them. Similarly, registrants who may not have received or neglected to return certain election office mailings were often removed from voter lists. In addition, clerical errors, such as erroneous changes of address or data entry errors in voter registration files, resulted in the loss of the opportunity to cast a ballot. The NVRA allows registered voters to vote when they move to another location within the registrar's jurisdiction [42 U.S.C. §1973gg-6]. Additional fail-safe voting requirements were incorporated into Federal law by the Help America Vote Act of 2002 (HAVA), which mandates the availability and use of provisional ballots under some circumstances.

Role of the United States Election Assistance Commission

Section 802(a) of HAVA (42 U.S.C. §15532(a)) transferred to EAC all functions that the Federal Election Commission (FEC) exercised under Section

9(a) of the NVRA. Pursuant to this authority, EAC has incorporated the FEC's NVRA survey instrument into a more comprehensive survey that addresses UOCAVA information and other topics that HAVA requests that EAC study. EAC's 2012 Election Administration and Voting Survey, also captured information on overseas voting, provisional ballots, voting technology, absentee voting, poll workers, and other issues. The data below are drawn from Section A.

SECTION 2. SURVEY BACKGROUND

This report addresses the impact of the National Voter Registration Act of 1993 (NVRA) (Pub. L. No. 10331, as amended, 42 U.S.C. §1973gg-1 et seq.) on the administration of elections for Federal office during the 2012 election cycle. These reports are submitted biennially pursuant to the provisions of the NVRA, as amended by HAVA. Section 9 of the NVRA provides, in part, as follows:

> SEC 9... (a) In general... the Election Assistance Commission...
>
> (3) not later than June 30 of each odd-numbered year, shall submit to the Congress a report assessing the impact of this Act on the administration of elections for Federal office during the preceding 2-year period and including recommendations for improvements in Federal and State procedures, forms, and other matters affected by this subchapter... (42 U.S.C. §1973gg-7(a)(3)).

This is the tenth NVRA report to Congress, it is the fifth submitted by EAC. The previous five reports were submitted by the FEC, which in 1994 promulgated rules identifying the information considered necessary to obtain from the States to generate reports to Congress (11 CFR §9428.7). The FEC described and explained the need for these data elements in a communication to State election officials in October 1995. With the passage of HAVA, the biennial survey and report were revised and expanded, and the survey has continued to evolve under EAC authority.

In 2012, as in 2010, EAC distributed two questionnaires to the States, the Statutory Overview and the Election Administration and Voting Survey (EAVS). In order to minimize the burden on States in preparing to respond to the survey, the 2012 survey contained only minor changes to both the Statutory Overview and the EAVS questionnaires from the 2010 versions. The final, approved version of the survey, posted on the EAC website in May 2012, contained 49 questions in the EAVS questionnaire and 22 questions in the Statutory Overview. A majority of the questions in both surveys contained sub-questions. The Statutory Overview and full EAVS questionnaires can be found at *www.eac.gov.*

In accordance with its statutory obligation to report on the impact of the NVRA on the administration of Federal elections, EAC submits this report to Congress. However, readers should note that since December 11, 2010, EAC has lacked a quorum of commissioners necessary to conduct certain business, including the issuing of recommendations in its reports. In order for EAC to meet its responsibility to submit the NVRA report to Congress by the statutory deadline, EAC provides in this document the information that would be contained in a formally adopted report. It is EAC staff's intention to submit this report to the Commission for ratification tally vote once a quorum has been reestablished.

States' Collection of NVRA Information

For 2012, EAC continued its effort to make the survey available to State officials earlier in the election cycle and to facilitate the task of responding by providing improved survey instruments and increased technical assistance. The primary survey instrument, designed to assist the States in collecting and reporting their statistical data, was a Microsoft Excel-based template. The template offered the States two different methods for entering data: a form-based method that resembled the look of the questionnaire, and a sheet-based view that used a familiar spreadsheet format. Embedded in the Microsoft Excel-based template was a set of error-checking algorithms using logic and consistency rules to help States check their data before submitting their data to EAC. To further ease the data entry burden, the template was preloaded with each State's jurisdictions and EAC provided a guide summarizing how to use the template to States.[7] Nearly all States chose to submit their data using this application. States submitted their data via the project web-site or by email.

EAC asked States to send their responses by February 1, 2013. The data provided by the States were then checked for logic and consistency errors. Any errors or questions concerning the submitted data were referred back to the States for review and correction, if necessary. The States had two weeks to review and correct their submissions. Fifty-four States submitted their data to EAC by the final deadline, March 1, 2013.[8]

About the States' Data

In May 2010, EAC adopted a data policy to guide States' submission and verification of their survey data. The Guide to the Election Administration and Voting Survey document provides information to election officials responsible for completing the survey and offers EAC assurances about States' validation of the data. The Guide is available on EAC's website (*www.eac.gov*). It contains information about:

- EAC processes related to releasing the survey instrument and final reports based on the survey data;
- The technical assistance EAC provides to the States;
- Deadlines for submitting the survey data;
- The processes and procedures for States' submission of the data, including use of the data templates EAC provides;
- The processes and procedures for States' review, verification, and correction of the data; and
- Instructions on how to address errors in the data after the submission deadline has passed.

In response to media and general public inquiries about State data cited in EAC's previous EAVS reports and the Federal government's recent policies related to data quality, EAC formally requests that States verify and certify in writing the data they submit. For the 2012 EAVS, every State submitted with their data a certification page signed by their Chief State Election Official.

States' method of data collection in preparing responses to the 2012 survey varied significantly. Most States relied, at least to some degree, upon centralized voter-registration databases (VRDs) and voter history databases, which allowed State election officials to respond to the survey with information from the local level for each question. Other States, however, collected relatively little election data at the State level and instead relied on cooperation from local jurisdiction election offices to complete the survey. States and local offices may have devoted different amounts of resources to data collection, and may have differed in the emphasis placed on data collection.

Some States did not provide data in all the sub-categories requested in the survey, and a few did not have data for all their local jurisdictions. When interpreting the data presented in this report, there is the possibility of missing data for an entire state on a given question or for some jurisdictions within

States; as such, the level of completeness varies across the survey questions. In reviewing the corresponding tables, it is important to review the "Cases" columns, which present the number of jurisdictions in each State able to respond to each survey question.

Section 3 of this report summarizes the results of the NVRA portion of the 2012 Election Administration and Voting Survey and includes a set of detailed tables. The corresponding dataset, that includes States' responses to the NVRA portion of the survey, is available on EAC's website (*www.eac.gov*).

Caution is necessary when interpreting the survey data, particularly when comparing the data from year-to-year or State-to-State, due to changes in State data collection practices across time and the varying levels of completeness in many States' responses. In 2006, EAC began asking States to produce county-level data (or the equivalent) rather than the statewide totals asked for previously. Even in States with centralized VRDs, some data may be kept only at the local level, and the level of integration of information between local and State election offices varies across the country. Information on the number of jurisdictions in each State is provided in a number of tables and summarized in Table 6.[9]

There are some State-level exceptions for the data that were collected. North Dakota does not have voter registration and is exempt from the NVRA; however, it elected to provide some data for this NVRA report. U.S. territories are not subject to the NVRA, and the States of Idaho, Minnesota, New Hampshire, Wisconsin, and Wyoming are exempt because they had Election Day Registration in 1994 and continuously thereafter.[10] These States and territories have an asterisk by their entries in the tables included in this report as a reminder that they are exempt from the NVRA (though some of these States chose to submit data anyway).

Some States did not track certain information requested by the survey, or they tracked it in ways that made answering parts of the survey difficult. For example, States may code their sources of registration applications differently than those asked for in the survey. Footnotes for each table provide further information on these issues. Finally, the national totals are not complete for all questions because of incomplete responses at the local and State level.

SECTION 3. SURVEY RESULTS

The data collected in the 2012 Election Administration and Voting Survey related to the NVRA are summarized below.

This section also describes the impact of the NVRA on the administration of elections for Federal offices for the 2012 election cycle.

Voter Registration

States reported that 194,198,928 voters were registered and eligible to cast ballots in the November 2012 presidential election. Approximately 79.9% of the nation's estimated voting age population of more than 243 million was registered for the 2012 election.[11]

Table 1c compares the States' registration rates with an estimate of the States' voting age population (VAP) from the U.S. Census Bureau.[12]

Since the VAP includes a significant number of persons who cannot vote, including non-citizens, a better picture of national registration rates can be obtained by using an estimate of citizen voting age population (CVAP). According to the EAC survey, 87.4% of the nation's approximately 222.3 million CVAP were registered for the 2012 election. Table 1d presents the registration rates for States compared with estimated CVAP. Note, however, that CVAP includes some ineligible voters, such as those who have lost their right to vote because of felony convictions or a designation of mental incompetency.[13]

The voting age population of the United States continues to increase at a rate of about one percent per year, according to estimates from the U.S. Census Bureau. The VAP increased from about 237,386,565 to about 243,003,673 during the 2012 election cycle, an increase of 2.4%.

This report contains data from all States and territories covered by HAVA except the Virgin Islands, but some important caveats are worth noting in terms of the number of registered voters North Dakota has no voter registration; for the purposes of this report, all people of voting age are considered registered in that State. Most States reported registration data for all jurisdictions.

A few States, however, reported only partial totals for some of the voter registration data because some county data were unavailable or some counties reported incomplete information; these cases are indicated in the tables and the table notes.

Active and Inactive Voters

The NVRA, which was not fully implemented until after the 1994 elections, prohibits the removal of names from the registration list solely for failure to vote.[14] The NVRA allows election jurisdictions to move voters to an inactive voter list if the registrant: (1) has not either notified the applicable registrar (in person or in writing) or responded during the period described in the statute, to the address confirmation notice sent by the applicable registrar; and subsequently(2) has not voted or appeared to vote in two or more consecutive general elections for Federal office.[15] Before moving voters to an inactive list, jurisdictions verify voter rolls through mailings or the U.S. Postal Service's National Change of Address (NCOA) service. This inactive status and the fail-safe provisions of the NVRA allow such people to vote if there was an error. As a result of the NVRA's requirement that States seek to remove ineligible voters from their registration rolls, most States have programs in place to verify their voter registration lists, but those verifications occur at different times and are performed in different ways.

States report their registration numbers for different purposes and in different ways.[16] EAC asked each State to report its number of "registered and eligible" voters and then asked for separate totals of active and inactive voters. In addition, the survey asked States how they reported the number of registered voters for "other official purposes." A total of 16 States responded that they only use active registered voters. Thirty States reported using active and inactive registered voters; seven States had some jurisdictions report using only active voters while other jurisdictions reported using both active and inactive voters. Since North Dakota does not have voter registration, it does not make a distinction between active and inactive voters. Furthermore, in 36 States, the number of "registered and eligible" voters for the November 2012 election equals precisely the number of inactive plus active voters.

Analysis of the change in the number of active voters is the most reliable indicator of the growth or decline in registration. Some States actually experienced a marked decrease in active registration despite the overall increase in reported registrations nationally. Excluding Kansas, which did not report counts of active and inactive voters, two States reported a decrease of over 10% in the number of active registrants since the 2010 elections: Michigan (-12.3%) and Ohio (-17.1%). In contrast, Florida reported an increase in active registration of 10.5%.

Responses to the 2012 survey show that over 23.1 million registrants in the United States remain on the list of inactive voters. California had the largest proportion of eligible voters on its inactive list—28.7%. Arkansas and Colorado were the other States with more than 20% of eligible voters on its inactive list. See Tables 1a and 1b for data on active and inactive voters for all 54 States.

Voter Registration Forms Received

Overall, 52 States reported receiving over 62.5 million voter registration forms during the 2012 election cycle (see Table 2a). The States reported sources for nearly 60.8 million registration forms, including the origin of new, duplicate, and invalid or rejected registrations (see Tables 2b, 2c and 2d).

The two largest sources of voter registration applications were (1) motor vehicle offices or (2) mail, fax, and email. Nearly 20.3 million applications, 32.4% of the total, were submitted to State offices that issued driver's licenses. Nearly 14.6 million, or 23.3% of applications, came from individual voters submitting applications by mail, fax, or email.[17] Individual voters who appeared in person to register at election offices made up another nearly 10.3 million applications, or 16.4%. Together, these three sources provided nearly three-fourths (72.2%) of all registration applications that States received. The remaining sources included Internet registration, public assistance offices, disability services offices, Armed Forces recruitment offices, registration drives from advocacy groups and political parties, and other State agencies.

In the 2012 election cycle the ratio of mail registrations to those coming from driver's license offices was similar to the last few mid-term election cycles but not to the last presidential election cycle. During the 2008 presidential election cycle, nearly as many voters registered through motor vehicle offices as the number of voters who registered by mail, fax, or email. During the 2012 presidential election cycle, however, registrations through motor vehicle offices were almost 40% higher than mail registrations. Similarly, the 2006 and 2010 mid-term election cycles had twice as many voters registered at motor vehicle offices than by mail, fax, or email.[18]

There was a substantial increase in the number of States that reported receiving voter registration applications directly over the Internet between 2008 and 2010, while there was a slight increase reported between 2010 and 2012.[19] In 2010, 17 States reported receiving voter registration applications directly over the Internet, up from eight States in 2008. In 2012, 21 States reported receiving a total of 3,329,216 applications over the Internet, a large increase from the 768,211 Internet applications received by States in 2010.

Arizona and California accounted for half of the total number of applications received from the Internet. Internet applications accounted for 49.3% of all applications processed in Arizona during the 2012 election cycle. Other States that reported receiving more than 10% of their applications from the Internet were Colorado (23.0%), California (13.8%), the District of Columbia (13.6%), Kansas (10.5%), Louisiana (10.4%), Nevada (10.4%), Oregon (25.1%), Utah (12.0%), and Washington (13.2%). The number of applications received through the Internet in most of the other States was small (often less than 5%). Although it is growing, outside of a handful of States, the use of the Internet as a direct means of registering to vote remains limited.

In accordance with EAC regulations, the 2012 survey asked States to break down the applications they received into three categories: new applications, duplicate applications, and invalid or rejected applications. There were over 23.8 million new applications reported by 53 States. Forty-five States reported receiving nearly 3.7 million duplicate applications of people already registered to vote. Forty-two States reported the number of invalid or rejected applications, totaling over 5 million.

Over one-third of the invalid applications (34.0%) came from mail applications, while another 12.8% came from in-person registrations at election offices. Registrations at driver's license offices, which comprised 32.4% of total applications, made up only 5.4% of invalid or rejected applications.

Voter Registration Forms Processed

States were asked to report on the kinds of applications they processed during the 2012 election cycle.

Of the 62.5 million applications received, 38.1%, or 23.8 million, were new, valid registrations. This represented at least 12.3% of the registered voters in the 2012 election. In addition, 33 States reported "pre-registering" 438,978 people under the age of 18, who would then become eligible to vote on their 18th birthday. Another 27.5 million applications, 44.0% of the 62.5 million received, were requests for a change in the address, name, or party of a voter already registered in the jurisdiction and another 3.7 million were requests for change of address across jurisdictions.

Forty-three States reported receiving approximately 3.7 million applications that were duplicates of existing registrations. Alaska and Hawaii reported that over 20% of applications received during the 2012 election cycle were duplicates. Nationwide, approximately 5 million, or 8.0% of applications, were rejected for a cause other than being a duplicate; some States had substantially higher rates. Indiana reported the highest rate, rejecting 43.0%, or 896,523, of applications for a cause other than duplication.[20]

Voter Registration List Maintenance

The NVRA prohibits States from removing names from the voter registration list for either of the following reasons:

- Failure to vote [42 U.S.C. §1973gg-6(b)(2)]; or
- Change of address to another location within the registrar's jurisdiction [42 U.S.C. §1973gg-6(f)]. The law requires registrars to update a registrant's voting address if they receive information on the registrant's change of address to another location within the registrar's jurisdiction.

The purpose of the list maintenance provisions of the NVRA is to ensure the accuracy and currency of the voter registration rolls. The Act states that any change of address submitted to a motor vehicle driver's license agency shall serve as notification of a change of address for voter registration unless the individual indicates that the change is not for voter registration purposes [42 U.S.C. §1973gg-3].

The law also requires States to conduct a uniform and nondiscriminatory general program [42 U.S.C. §1973gg-6(a) (4)] to remove the names of ineligible voters, as follows:

- Upon the death of the registrant;
- Upon the registrant's written confirmation that his or her address has changed to a location outside the registrar's jurisdiction; or
- On the registrant's failure to respond to certain confirmation mailings along with failure to appear to vote in two consecutive Federal general elections subsequent to the mailing. (The confirmation mailings in this case are those mailed out to registrants who, based on information received from the Postal Service, have apparently changed address to a location outside the registrar's jurisdiction.)

The NVRA also permits States to remove the names of registrants as follows:

- On the request of the registrant [42 U.S.C. §1973gg-6(a)(3) (A)];
- For mental incapacity of the registrant, as provided for in State law [42 U.S.C. §1973gg-6(a)(3)(B)]; or
- On criminal conviction of the registrant, as provided for in State law [42 U.S.C. §1973gg-6(a)(3)(B)].

Other than these provisions, the law grants States wide latitude as to when, where, and how these functions will be performed. Two tables at the end of this report (Table 4a, Voter List Maintenance: Confirmation Notices, and Table 4b, Voter List Maintenance: Removal Actions) provide data from the 2012 EAVS on the number of confirmation notices sent during the 2012 election cycle, the number of responses received from those notices, the number of registrants who were moved from active to inactive status on the voter lists, and the number of registrants who were removed from the voter lists. The tables also provide data on the reasons why registrants were removed from the voter lists, including death, failure to vote, a disqualifying felony conviction, and at the voter's request.

Confirmation Notices

Confirmation notices are an important tool for the maintenance of accurate voter registration rolls. The 43 States that responded to this portion of the survey reported sending out over 17.5 million confirmation notices during the 2012 election cycle (Table 4a). The ratio of confirmation notices to number of registered voters was 9.0% nationally and varied significantly across the States. Two States sent out significantly more confirmation notices, relative to their total voter registration, than other States: Arizona sent out over 3.6 million confirmation notices, equal to 98.0% of its total registration;[21] and Colorado sent out over 1.3 million, equal to 35.7% of its total registration.

There were large differences across the States in reported response to confirmation notices. Voters confirmed their registration in response to only about 17.8% of confirmation notices sent, approximately 3.1 million, although this is likely an underestimate as some States did not provide data on the number of responses received. Another 3.9% of voters, or 687,092, confirmed that they should be deleted from the rolls, although this percentage is also likely an underestimate given missing data. In contrast, Delaware reported that voters responded to almost all of the notices (99.9%) and 16 other States reported response rates greater than 20%.

States reported that approximately 2.9 million, or 16.3% of confirmation notices, were returned undeliverable, leaving another 6.8 million, or 38.8% of notices, with status unknown. North Carolina (55.2%), South Dakota (44.4%), and Illinois (41.0%) had high rates of notices that were not deliverable. States either reported the resolution of the rest of the confirmation notices in miscellaneous categories or did not report what happened to the notices, suggesting that better tracking of confirmation notices may be needed to provide a more complete picture.

Removal from Voter Rolls

Nearly 13.7 million voters were removed from registration rolls in the two years leading up to the 2012 presidential election (see Table 4b). Forty-nine States provided data on their removal of voters from registration rolls. The number of voters removed during the 2012 election cycle was larger than the number of removals in the 2008 election cycle, even though only two more States reported data. In the 2008 election cycle, approximately 12.6 million registrants from 47 States were removed.

States varied in the number of people removed relative to total registration. Fifteen States reported removing at least 10% of their 2012 registration, with New Hampshire reported removing over 20% of their 2012 registration. Overall, States removed 7.1% of registered voters in 2012.

Of the nearly 13.7 million voters removed from the rolls, over 3.7 million, or 27.1%, were removed because they moved to other jurisdictions; Maine had the highest percentage of removals due to moving at 60.6%. Overall, nearly 3.0 million voters, or 21.6% of all voters removed, were removed because they had died.

The leading cause of removal of inactive voters was a failure to respond to a confirmation notice *and* subsequent failure to vote in the two most recent Federal elections, accounting for 4.1 million voters, or 30.1% of the total removals. However, this is a drastic decrease from the 6.1 million voters removed for this reason in 2010. These removals represented greater than 80% of removals in New Hampshire and Wyoming in 2012. Felony conviction—a disqualifier in many States—removed 308,797 voters from the rolls, representing 2.3% of removals. In Florida, 39.8% of removals were due to felony convictions.[22] Other reasons for removing voters from the rolls included requests by voters (2.5% of all removals) and mental incompetence (0.1%).

Election Day Registration[23]

EAC asked States to provide information on voters who register to vote and cast their ballots on the same day. Voters are able to register and vote on the same day in varying ways, and the question was phrased in an attempt to capture all those voters who register and vote on the same day. Some States have formal same-day voting systems, while others limit same-day voting to certain contests or certain groups of voters. For example, Alaska limits Election Day registrants to voting only for Federal offices. Other States have special registration and voting provisions for new residents or recently discharged military. Finally, some States experience overlaps between early voting periods and the cutoff date for registration. Data from this question are presented in Table 5.

EAC asked a question to distinguish between States that had Election Day or Same Day Registration in 2012 and States that did not have Election Day Registration, but allowed voters to register and vote on the same day in that election. Twelve States including Alaska, the District of Columbia, Idaho, Iowa, Maine, Minnesota, Montana, New Hampshire, North Carolina, Rhode Island, Wisconsin, and Wyoming indicated that they had Election Day Registration or Same Day Registration for the November 2012 presidential election. California, Colorado, Mississippi, New Mexico, Ohio, Oregon, Vermont, and Washington reported a number of voters who were allowed to register and then to vote on the same day, but did not indicate why this was the case.

For 2012, the 20 States listed above reported that nearly 1.4 million new registration applications were filed on days in which it was possible to both register and vote. In Idaho, New Hampshire, and Wyoming, Same Day Registration accounted for more than 10% of reported registration in 2012, and approximately 30% of total applications received during the 2012 election cycle. Same Day Registration was also more than 20% of total applications in Maine and Minnesota. Approximately 80.8% of new Election Day Registration applications were from the 12 States that reported having Election Day or Same Day Registration.

SECTION 4. OBSERVATIONS

In recent years changes to State voter registration systems have been significant. Seeking to improve the way in which voter registration applications are received, processed, and maintained, HAVA required States to implement statewide voter registration lists by January 1, 2004.[24] The process of improving the nation's voter registration system continues, and EAC offers the following observations to Congress and to State and local election officials as they continue to improve their systems in compliance with HAVA, the NVRA, and other State and Federal election laws.

States should continue to improve and modernize their electronic reporting and list maintenance systems.

States are encouraged to use their statewide databases as tools for generating data to assist them with responding to the NVRA section of EAC's Election Administration and Voting Survey and other requests for data. Electronic databases help ease the burden of responding to such requests for State and local officials alike. The 2012 report shows better data collection and reporting efforts on the part of States, and most were able to report the statewide totals, however challenges remain with collecting certain voter registration data.

While most States were able to report the number of registration applications received, some States had difficulty providing data for select subcategories, such as number of applications received through the State motor vehicles department or Public Assistance offices. Additionally, some States could not report the number of confirmation notices sent to voters, while many had difficulty producing data related to the disposition of those notices. Still others could not report the number of invalid or rejected registrations. In the States where non-reporting exists, States experienced difficulties in getting the requested data from their local jurisdictions. States are encouraged to continue working with their local officials to develop an efficient process for tracking and submitting data electronically so that States are able to submit the most complete set of data possible.

States should continue to engage their State agencies on issues related to the NVRA and to encourage those agencies to remind voters to check and update their voter registration information.

States should encourage departments of motor vehicles, public assistance and disability service agencies, along with other public services agencies or organizations with which they work to distribute voter registration forms, and to remind voters to check and to update their registration information. Developing an on-going relationship with State public service agencies around NVRA requirements will help ensure that citizens are able to take advantage of all voter registration opportunities available to them.

End Notes

[1] The six States are Idaho, Minnesota, New Hampshire, North Dakota, Wisconsin, and Wyoming. These States and the four territories are marked with an asterisk in the tables as a reminder that they are exempt from the NVRA.

[2] Throughout this report, the word "States" includes "States, territories, and the District of Columbia."

[3] While data for 2008, 2010, and 2012 are cited for illustrative purposes throughout this report, the 2008 and 2012 elections were presidential elections, which make them more comparable.

[4] It is important to note that some of these differences may be due in part to changes in the accuracy and completeness of data provided in 2008 and 2010

[5] Implementing the National Voter Registration Act of 1993: Requirements, Issues, Approaches, and Examples, prepared by the National Clearinghouse on Election Administration, Federal Election Commission, Washington, DC, 1994 (FEC Guide, page I-1).

[6] The NVRA allows States to designate other State offices for voter registration, including public libraries, city and county clerks' offices, public schools, and fishing and hunting license bureaus (Pub. L. No. 103-31, as amended, 42 U.S.C. §1973gg-5).

[7] States were allowed to change the list of jurisdictions to match their own reporting and administration systems. Some States, particularly those with township systems, may change the number of local jurisdictions administering elections from year to year, as towns run joint elections to ease the administrative burden.

[8] The Virgin Islands was the only jurisdiction that did not respond. Its name appears in the tables but without any data.

[9] States were given the option of answering "data not available" and, for some questions, "data not applicable." The "cases" columns provided in the tables report all local jurisdictions in which a State responded with a number, whether zero or higher. In some cases, States may have responded zero instead of "data not available" or "data not applicable," or vice versa. A blank cell in the table could represent missing data or the selection of "data not available" or "data not applicable" across all jurisdictions in the State. The "States Included" rows report the number of States in which a State responded with a number, whether zero or higher. Complete data for the NVRA section of the survey can be downloaded at www.eac.gov.

[10] § 42 USC 1973gg-2(b)

[11] EAC uses the U.S. Census Bureau's estimate of voting age population for the number of voters registered to vote in North Dakota for purposes of this report because North Dakota does not have voter registration.

[12] States were asked to provide the number of voters "eligible and registered" at the time of the Federal election. In reality, this number is an estimate in some States and not applicable in others.

[13] The Bureau of the Census provides information from which an approximation of the Citizen Voting Age Population (CVAP) may be obtained. The estimate for CVAP has been derived from the 2011 three-year ACS data. It is applied to the 2012 VAP to estimate CVAP for 2012. See Table 1d for more details.

[14] 42 U.S.C. §1973gg–6(b)(2)

[15] 42 U.S.C. §1973gg-6(d)

[16] See the "Voter Registration File Maintenance" section of this report (on pages 2 to 3) for a discussion of the NVRA's treatment of active and inactive voters.

[17] The Table 2 column header is labeled mail registration applications, but the entire subcategory includes mail, fax, and email.

[18] States may have counted their sources of applications differently. For example, 31 States reported figures for third-party voter registration drives by advocacy groups or political parties separately; other States included such drives in their totals for in-person or mail applications.

[19] States vary in their definition of Internet (or online) voter registration. Some States define it as offering a fillable PDF; for others, it includes the ability to email the registration form. The 2012 Statutory Overview results indicated that during the 2012 election cycle, 11 States offered online voter registration and 38 States offered a voter registration form online that voters could download and complete, with most requiring the form to be submitted by mail or in-person. For more information, see EAC's 2012 Statutory Overview report, available at www.eac.gov.

[20] The survey did not ask States to provide the reasons for these rejections.

[21] Note that in Maricopa County, a mass confirmation mailing was sent to all voters on file in 2012, accounting for the large majority of confirmation notices sent in the State.

[22] Results from the 2012 Statutory Overview indicate that fifty-one States disenfranchise felons in some manner. Some States restore voting rights after unconditional discharge or a specified period of time. For more details, see the 2012 Statutory Overview report, available at www.eac.gov.

[23] As used here, and in the survey, Election Day Registration refers to any day (prior to and including Election Day itself) when eligible voters could register and cast their ballots on the same day. Because of the question's wording, data were collected from some States that do not consider themselves to have Election Day Registration.

[24] States obtaining a waiver could postpone implementation until 2006.

In: National Voter Registration Act

Editor: Aaliyah Garner

ISBN: 978-1-63117-829-0

© 2014 Nova Science Publishers, Inc.

Chapter 3

THE UNIFORMED AND OVERSEAS CITIZENS ABSENTEE VOTING ACT: OVERVIEW AND ISSUES[*]

Kevin J. Coleman

SUMMARY

Members of the uniformed services and U.S. citizens who live abroad are eligible to register and vote absentee in federal elections under the Uniformed and Overseas Citizens Absentee Voting Act (UOCAVA, P.L. 99-410) of 1986. The law was enacted to improve absentee registration and voting for this group of voters and to consolidate existing laws. Since 1942, a number of federal laws have been enacted to assist these voters: the Soldier Voting Act of 1942 (P.L. 77-712, amended in 1944), the Federal Voting Assistance Act of 1955 (P.L. 84-296), the Overseas Citizens Voting Rights Act of 1975 (P.L. 94-203; both the 1955 and 1975 laws were amended in 1978 to improve procedures), and the Uniformed and Overseas Citizens Absentee Voting Act of 1986. The law is administered by the Secretary of Defense, who delegates that responsibility to the director of the Federal Voting Assistance Program (FVAP) at the Department of Defense (DOD).

Improvements to UOCAVA were necessary as the result of controversy surrounding ballots received in Florida from uniformed services and

---

[*] This is an edited, reformatted and augmented version of Congressional Research Service Publication, No. RS20764, dated February 20, 2014.

overseas voters in the 2000 presidential election. The National Defense Authorization Act for FY2002 (P.L. 107-107) and the Help America Vote Act of 2002 (P.L. 107-252) both included provisions concerning uniformed services and overseas voting. The Ronald W. Reagan Defense Authorization Act for FY2005 (P.L. 108-375) amended UOCAVA as well, and the John Warner National Defense Authorization Act for FY2007 (P.L. 109-364) extended a DOD program to assist UOCAVA voters.

In the 111th Congress, a major overhaul of UOCAVA was completed when President Obama signed the National Defense Authorization Act for FY2010 (P.L. 111-84) on October 28, 2009. It included an amendment (S.Amdt. 1764) that contained the provisions of S. 1415, the Military and Overseas Voter Empowerment Act (the MOVE Act).

In July 2013, the Election Assistance Commission issued its report on UOCAVA voting in the general election of 2012. The biennial report is mandated by the Help America Vote Act. According to the results, ballots were transmitted to UOCAVA voters by election officials in all 50 states and several territories, but nearly half of all ballots were sent from California, Florida, New York, Texas, and Washington. The rate of ballots returned for counting was higher than in 2010, but lower than in the presidential election of 2008. States counted 95.8% of the ballots that were returned.

Several relevant bills have been introduced in the 113th Congress, including H.R. 12, H.R. 1655, H.R. 2168, H.R. 3576, S. 123, S. 1034, and S. 1728. The Senate Committee on Rules and Administration held a hearing on S. 1728 on January 29, 2014.

HISTORICAL OVERVIEW

Federal efforts to assist members of the Armed Forces date to 1864, when President Abraham Lincoln issued an order to allow members of the military to return home to cast a ballot if they could not vote absentee according to the laws of their respective states.[1] Eighteen states, all in the North, permitted soldiers to vote absentee by establishing remote voting at military encampments where units were usually organized by state. Some other states permitted an absent military voter to designate a proxy, who would cast a ballot, as directed, on the voter's behalf.[2]

Little progress occurred concerning absentee voting by members of the military in the following decades, despite an expansion of state absentee voting laws. Such laws generally extended absentee voting rights to those absent from their voting district, but who were permitted to send an absentee ballot by mail from within the state. Even those state laws designed specifically to assist absent military voters either did not apply to overseas soldiers, or were ineffective because of the barriers to delivering and receiving mail in overseas locations. When the issue arose for overseas soldiers in World War I, the War Department announced that "it would not conduct or supervise the taking of the service vote," but pledged cooperation with the states that could establish their own means to do so.[3] A contradictory statement noted that the "soldier vote could not be taken in France or on other foreign soil in the theater of war without serious interference with military efficiency," and, in the end, "no states were allowed to poll the vote of soldiers on foreign soil."[4] Likewise, the first federal legislation to assist military voters was introduced in 1918, but was not acted upon. The issue subsided until World War II, when the challenge of how to facilitate military voting—especially by those stationed overseas—emerged once again.

The first federal absentee voting law was the Soldier Voting Act of 1942 (P.L. 77-712) that guaranteed the right to vote in federal elections to members of the Armed Forces who were absent from their places of residence during wartime. The law allowed members of the Armed Forces to vote for presidential electors and candidates for the U.S. Senate and House, whether or not they were previously registered and regardless of poll tax requirements. The law provided for the use of a postage-free, federal post card application to request an absentee ballot; it also instructed secretaries of state to prepare an appropriate number of "official war ballots," which listed federal office candidates, as well as candidates for state and local office if authorized by the state legislature. The law "had almost no impact at all" with respect to assisting Armed Forces voters, or on the outcome of the election itself, because it was enacted on September 16, only weeks before the 1942 November general election.[5] Only 28,000 of 5 million soldiers voted that year.[6]

Under congressional war powers, the 1942 law *mandated* procedures for the states to permit service members to vote, but the law as amended in 1944 *recommended* that states follow such procedures. Congressional authority to regulate state voting procedures expired once the war ended, because the law noted that its provisions applied "in time of war."[7] The law was amended again in 1946 to include technical changes.

In 1951, President Truman asked the American Political Science Association (APSA) to study the military voting problem and make recommendations. APSA completed its study in 1952 and the President endorsed the association's legislative recommendations, which were sent to

Congress. The Federal Voting Assistance Act (P.L. 84-296) was subsequently enacted in 1955; it recommended, but did not guarantee, absentee registration and voting for members of the military, federal employees who lived outside the United States, and members of civilian service organizations affiliated with the Armed Forces. The law was amended in 1968 to include a more general provision for U.S. citizens temporarily residing outside the United States, expanding the number of civilians covered under the law. The Overseas Citizens Voting Rights Act of 1975 (P.L. 94-203) guaranteed absentee registration and voting rights for citizens outside the United States, whether or not they maintained a U.S. residence or address and whether or not they intended to return.

SUMMARY OF THE CURRENT LAW

The current law, the Uniformed and Overseas Citizens Absentee Voting Act (P.L. 99-410), was signed into law by President Reagan on August 28, 1986.[8] It consolidated the provisions of the Federal Voting Assistance Act of 1955 that pertained to military voters and their dependents, and the Overseas Citizens Voting Rights Act of 1975 that pertained to American citizens abroad. The law was amended by the Help America Vote Act (P.L. 107-252) in 2002, the National Defense Authorization Act of 2002 (P.L. 107-107), the Defense Authorization Act for FY2005 (P.L. 108- 375), the John Warner National Defense Authorization Act for FY2007 (P.L. 109-364), and the National Defense Authorization Act for FY2010 (P.L. 111-84). The main provisions of the law require states to do the following:

- Permit uniformed services voters,[9] their spouses and dependents, and overseas voters who no longer maintain a residence in the United States to register absentee (overseas voters are eligible to register absentee in the jurisdiction of their last residence) and to vote by absentee ballot in all elections for federal office (including general, primary, special, and runoff elections).[10] The National Defense Authorization Act of 2002 amended UOCAVA to permit a voter to submit a single absentee application in order to receive an absentee ballot for each federal election in the state during the year. The Help America Vote Act subsequently amended that section of the law to extend the period covered by a single absentee ballot application to the next two regularly scheduled general elections for federal office.

The section was repealed in 2009 under the National Defense Authorization Act for FY2010. The Help America Vote Act also added a new section that prohibits a state from refusing to accept a valid voter registration application on the grounds that it was submitted prior to the first date on which the state processes applications for the year; this section was retained when the law was amended in 2009.[11]

- Accept and process any valid voter registration application from an absent uniformed services voter or overseas voter if the application is received not less than 30 days before the election. The Help America Vote Act amended that section of the law to require a state to provide to a voter the reasons for rejecting a registration application or an absentee ballot request.[12]

- The law recommends that states accept the federal write-in absentee ballot for general elections for federal office (provided the voter is registered, has made a timely request for a state absentee ballot, the absentee ballot has not arrived with sufficient time to return it, and the ballot is submitted from outside the United States or its territories).[13]

- The law also stipulates that voting materials be carried "expeditiously and free of postage."[14] It recommends that states accept the Federal Post Card Application (FPCA) from uniformed services voters, their spouses and dependents, and overseas voters, to allow for simultaneous absentee registration and to request an absentee ballot. While all states and territories accept the FPCA, some require that a voter submit the state registration form separately in order to be permanently registered. Other recommendations in the law suggest that states:[15]

  - waive registration requirements for military and overseas voters who do not have an opportunity to register because of service or residence;
  - send registration materials, along with an absentee ballot to be returned simultaneously, if the FPCA is not sufficient for absentee registration;
  - expedite the processing of voting materials;
  - permit any required oath to be administered by a commissioned officer in the military or by any official authorized to administer oaths under federal law or the law of the state where the oath is administered;

- assure mailing absentee ballots to military and overseas voters at the earliest opportunity; and
- provide for late registration for persons recently separated from the military.

In addition to the amendments to UOCAVA mentioned above, the Help America Vote Act of 2002 did the following:

- required the Secretary of Defense to establish procedures to provide time and resources for voting action officers to perform voting assistance duties; established procedures to ensure a postmark or proof of mailing date on absentee ballots; required secretaries of the Armed Forces to notify members of the last day for which ballots mailed at the facility can be expected to reach state or local officials in a timely fashion; required that members of the military and their dependents have access to information on registration and voting requirements and deadlines; and required that each person who enlists receives the national voter registration form;
- amended UOCAVA to require each state to designate a single office to provide information to all absent uniformed services voters and overseas voters who wish to register in the state;
- amended UOCAVA to require states to report the number of ballots sent to uniformed services and overseas voters and the number returned and cast in the election; and
- amended UOCAVA to require the Secretary of Defense to ensure that state officials are aware of the requirements of the law and to prescribe a standard oath for voting materials to be used in states that require such an oath.

The Defense Authorization Act for FY2002 also included provisions that (1) required an annual review of the voting assistance program and a report to Congress; (2) guaranteed state residency for military personnel who are absent because of military duty; (3) continued the online voting pilot project begun for the 2000 elections; and (4) permitted the use of DOD facilities as polling places if they had previously been used for that purpose since 1996 or were designated for use by December 2000.

The Ronald W. Reagan National Defense Authorization Act of Fiscal Year 2005 (P.L. 108-375) amended UOCAVA to permit absent military voters in the United States to use the federal write-in ballot, previously intended for use only by overseas voters. It repealed the requirement to continue the electronic voting demonstration project for the November 2004 election by delaying continuation of the program until the Election Assistance Commission has established appropriate guidelines and certifies that it will assist in carrying out the project. Finally, it required a report from the Secretary of Defense within 60 days of enactment on actions taken to ensure effective functioning of Federal Voting Assistance Program with respect to members of the Armed Forces deployed in support of Operation Iraqi Freedom, Operation Enduring Freedom, and other contingency operations.

The John Warner National Defense Authorization Act for Fiscal Year 2007 (P.L. 109-364) extended the Interim Voting Assistance System (IVAS) ballot request program through the end of 2006 and required the Comptroller General to assess DOD programs to facilitate UOCAVA voting, including progress on an Internet-based voting system.

Provisions of the Military and Overseas Voter Empowerment Act

The latest revision of UOCAVA, the Military and Overseas Voter Empowerment Act (MOVE Act), was signed into law by President Obama on October 28, 2009, as part of the National Defense Authorization Act for FY2010 (P.L. 111-84). The Senate had approved the conference committee report (H.Rept. 111-288) on the defense authorization act (H.R. 2647) on October 22 and the House had done so on October 8. The law's provisions included the following:

- States are required to establish procedures to permit absent uniformed services voters and overseas voters to request voter registration and absentee ballot applications by mail and electronically for all federal elections.
- States are required to establish procedures to transmit, by mail and electronically, blank absentee ballots to absent uniformed services voters and overseas voters for federal elections.
- States are required to transmit a validly requested absentee ballot to an absent uniformed services voter or overseas voter no later than 45 days before an election if the request is received at least 45 days before the election. A state can seek a hardship waiver from the requirement under certain circumstances.

- The presidential designee who administers the law (Secretary of Defense) is required to establish procedures to collect marked general election absentee ballots from absent overseas uniformed services voters for delivery to the appropriate election official.
- The use of the federal write-in absentee ballot for general elections has been broadened to include special, primary, and runoff elections as well.
- A state is prohibited from refusing to accept an otherwise valid voter registration application, absentee ballot application or marked absentee ballot from an absent uniformed services or overseas voter on the basis of notarization requirements or restrictions on paper or envelope type, including size and weight.
- The presidential designee is required to develop online portals of information to inform absent uniformed services voters about voter registration and absentee ballot procedures and make other improvements to the Federal Voting Assistance Program.
- The presidential designee is required to develop standards for states to report on the number of absentee ballots transmitted to and received from absent uniformed services and overseas voters and to develop standards to store such data.
- The act repeals subsections of the Uniformed and Overseas Citizens Absentee Voting Act (UOCAVA) which required states to process an official post card form as an absentee ballot request for the next two regularly scheduled general elections, if requested by the voter. The act would retain the subsection that prohibits a state from refusing to accept or process an otherwise valid registration or absentee ballot application because it was submitted before the date on which the state accepts such applications from absentee voters who are not members of the armed services.
- The presidential designee is required to report to relevant committees in Congress on the implementation of the program to collect and deliver marked ballots from overseas uniformed services voters and to assess the Voting Assistance Officer program at the Department of Defense.
- The Attorney General is required to submit an annual report to Congress on any civil action brought with respect to UOCAVA during the preceding year.
- The act authorizes requirements payments under the Help America Vote Act to meet the new requirements of the act.

- The presidential designee may establish one or more pilot programs to test new election technology to assist absent uniformed services and overseas voters.

Move Act Implementation

Most of the provisions of the MOVE Act were effective as of the November 2, 2010, general election. According to the National Conference of State Legislatures (NCSL), 24 states enacted legislation to comply with the new law or certain provisions of it in 2010.[16] A pressing issue for states that had late-occurring primaries was the requirement for absentee ballots to be mailed 45 days before a federal election. Hawaii's primary date was September 18, which was 45 days before the general election, and seven other states and the District of Columbia had primaries scheduled for the 14th of September, 49 days before the election (Delaware, Maryland, Massachusetts, New Hampshire, New York, Rhode Island, and Wisconsin). Preparing and printing general election absentee ballots may take longer than several days for a number of reasons. Delays in tabulating results are not uncommon, and the results must often be certified or otherwise validated before the names of winning candidates can be included on general election ballots. Election contests can cause further delays. States that changed the primary date in order to achieve compliance with the 45-day ballot availability requirement include Minnesota (August 10) and Vermont (August 24). In Hawaii, a bill to move the primary to the second Saturday in August was approved and signed by the governor, but it did not become effective until January 2011.

A state could obtain a waiver from the 45-day ballot availability requirement if (1) the primary date prevents the state from complying, (2) a legal contest results in a delay in generating the absentee ballots or, (3) the state constitution prevents compliance. Twelve jurisdictions applied for a waiver based on the date of the primary, including Alaska (August 24), Colorado (August 10), Delaware, the District of Columbia, Hawaii, Maryland, Massachusetts, New York, Rhode Island, the Virgin Islands (September 11), Wisconsin, and Washington (August 17). The Department of Defense issued a press release on August 27 announcing that waiver requests had been approved for five states (Delaware, Massachusetts, New York, Rhode Island, and Washington), and not approved for six jurisdictions (Alaska, Colorado, Hawaii, the Virgin Islands, Wisconsin, and the District of Columbia).[17] Maryland withdrew its waiver application on August 25, 2010. A few days before the general election, the state was ordered by U.S. District Judge Roger Titus to extend the deadline for receiving marked ballots from November 12 to

November 22.[18] Maryland reportedly sent ballots that listed federal candidates only, in order to comply with the 45-day ballot availability deadline in the MOVE Act. A member of the Maryland National Guard sued the state board of elections, alleging that the state's actions denied overseas voters sufficient time to vote for state candidates (i.e., governor).

Department of Justice Enforcement

With respect to enforcement, the Department of Justice filed lawsuits against a number of states to ensure that overseas military and civilian voters could fully participate in the November 2 election under the new MOVE Act provisions. The department also drew criticism with respect to its enforcement efforts, as some observers asserted that it had not moved quickly or forcefully enough to ensure that all states would be in compliance for the election.[19] In September 2010, the department filed suit against Wisconsin, and it subsequently filed suit the following month against Guam, Illinois, New York, and New Mexico. Wisconsin and the department reached an agreement (at the same time as the lawsuit was filed) under which the state would accept absentee ballots until November 19 and local election officials would send ballots no later than October 1.[20] The department filed suit against Guam in early October in federal district court in Hagatna, Guam, and also sought emergency relief to extend the deadline for accepting absentee ballots until November 15 and require officials to ensure email delivery of blank ballots.[21] The suit went to trial and Guam was ordered by the federal judge to extend the deadline until November 15.[22] In Illinois, various county election officials failed to send ballots by September 18 and also failed to send ballots electronically to voters who had requested that means of delivery; the ballots were instead sent by mail. The department reached an agreement with Illinois—announced on October 22—under which the state would extend the deadline for receiving voted ballots until November 16 (in six counties), extended the date such ballots must be postmarked from November 1 to November 2, and required counties to send ballots electronically to voters who had requested them. The department announced that it had reached an agreement with New Mexico on October 13; the lawsuit had alleged that election officials in six counties had violated federal law when they failed to send absentee ballots to military and overseas voters by September 18. The agreement extended the deadline for accepting ballots that were requested by September 18 from November 2 to November 6.[23] New York had received a waiver on August 27, provided ballots were transmitted by October 1 and accepted for counting until November 15 for ballots postmarked by

November 1. Thirteen counties failed to send ballots by October 1 and the department subsequently filed suit against the state, as well as the State Board of Elections. The parties subsequently signed a consent decree that required extending the deadline for receipt of ballots postmarked by November 1 until November 24. The state was also to make efforts to notify voters of these changes and that they could receive ballots electronically through the state's online ballot delivery wizard. A report on the number of ballots sent, returned, and counted must be filed after the election.[24]

With respect to other states that had difficulty meeting the requirement, Alaska, Colorado, the District of Columbia, Hawaii, Kansas, Mississippi, Nevada, North Dakota, and the Virgin Islands each entered into a memorandum of agreement with the Department of Justice concerning the requirement. Under a consent decree issued by the U.S. District Court for the Western District of Wisconsin, the state had agreed to certify the September 14 primary results by September 27 and ordered local election officials to transmit absentee ballots no later than October 1; the state would accept voted ballots that were executed and sent by November 2 and received by November 19 (Wisconsin's deadline for accepting UOCAVA ballots was 10 days after the general election).[25] Alaska expedited its certification of results so that ballots could be prepared by September 18; requests from voters for ballots to be faxed to them would be sent on that day as well.[26] Colorado agreed to "take all necessary actions" to ensure that each of its 64 counties transmitted ballots by September 18, to deploy staff from the Secretary of State's office to assist in that endeavor, and to notify the Department of Justice of any failure to do so.[27] The District of Columbia agreed to complete certification of the September 14 primary results by September 24, to make ballots available for transmission to UOCAVA voters no later than October 4, and extended the deadline for accepting such ballots by seven days until November 19 (the District's deadline for accepting UOCAVA ballots is 10 days after the election).[28] Hawaii agreed to send ballots no later than September 24 (barring election contests), and to use express delivery and return of ballots that had been requested by mail.[29] In Kansas, seven counties failed to send ballots by September 18 and the state agreed to extend the deadline for accepting ballots to ensure a 45-day period to vote an absentee ballot. The state would also provide contact information for voters who needed assistance and would file a report on the number of ballots received and counted.[30] Mississippi reached a similar agreement when 22 of its counties failed to send ballots in time to meet the requirement. Ballot acceptance deadlines were to be extended to November 8, in cases where the ballot request was received by September 18, and the state would notify voters of the extension and provide a post-election report.[31] One county in Nevada failed to send ballots to 34 voters who had requested them by September 18, and the state agreed to extend the county deadline for accepting ballots until November 8, provided they were executed and sent by election day.[32] The Virgin Islands had one federal office on the general election ballot, for which there was no primary election. These ballots were to be sent no later than September 18. A second ballot with local candidates was to be sent by October 2, after the primary results have been certified.[33]

A second issue concerned the new requirement for states to establish procedures to allow UOCAVA voters to request registration and absentee ballot applications electronically and by mail, and for states to transmit the materials to the voter in the same manner. It was unclear how many states either did not provide for electronic means of submission or delivery, or did so only under certain circumstances.[34] With respect to returning marked ballots, 19 states, American Samoa, Guam, and Puerto Rico permitted voters to return ballots by mail only. Thirty one states and the Virgin Islands permitted voters to return ballots by mail and fax and, in some cases, by email as well.

The Department of Justice enforces UOCAVA and the MOVE Act included a provision that requires the Attorney General to submit an annual report to Congress (by December 31) on any civil action pursued with respect to its enforcement of the law. In its 2010 report, the department outlined its enforcement efforts regarding the MOVE Act and noted that, in April 2010, it had "sent letters to all covered jurisdictions reminding them of the MOVE Act's requirements and requesting information about their plans for complying with the law."[35]

THE FEDERAL VOTING ASSISTANCE PROGRAM

The Federal Voting Assistance Act of 1955 called for the President to designate the head of an executive department to be responsible for and coordinate the federal functions described in the law. President Eisenhower designated the Secretary of Defense, who delegated the responsibility to the Assistant Secretary of Defense for Public Affairs, as coordinator of the Federal Voting Assistance Program (FVAP). Under the current law, the director of the Federal Voting Assistance Program administers the FVAP for citizens covered by the Uniformed and Overseas Citizens Absentee Voting Act. This office publishes a print and online version of its *Voting Assistance Guide*, a compilation of state requirements and practices with respect to the federal law.[36] The FVAP office also maintains a toll free phone number to provide assistance to voters and to military and federal government personnel who are responsible for implementing the law; the office also maintains a website at http://www.fvap.gov. The website includes a fully electronic system for uniformed services and overseas voters to register, request a ballot, and track the ballot for all voting jurisdictions in the country.

FVAP Programs Since 2000 to Promote Voting Participation

Voting over the Internet (VOI)

In the 2000 presidential general election, some members of the military and citizens living abroad cast their votes via the Internet on November 7. Voters who were covered by the UOCAVA and whose legal residence was one of 14 counties participating in the project in Florida, South Carolina, Texas, and Utah were eligible to participate. The program, referred to as the Voting Over the Internet (VOI) pilot project, was limited to a total of 350 potential voters who could request and vote an absentee ballot via the Internet. The project was designed to explore the viability of using the Internet to assist UOCAVA voters, most of whom face unique challenges when registering and voting. To request a ballot, the voter would fill out an electronic version of the request form and sign it with a digital certificate. A local election official would then post an electronic version of the ballot to a secure server, where it would be retrieved by the voter. Once the ballot was completed by the voter, it was digitally signed and encrypted and placed on a FVAP server. The completed ballot could only be decrypted by the appropriate local election official, who printed the ballot and counted it with mail-in absentee ballots. A total of 91 persons used the system to register to vote and 84 (representing 21 states and territories, and 11 countries) cast ballots under the program. A report that evaluated the program was issued in June 2001 by FVAP and noted, among other conclusions, that "further development is needed before Internet remote registration and voting can be provided effectively, reliably, and securely on a large scale."[37]

Secure Electronic Registration and Voting Experiment (SERVE)

An expanded version of the VOI project was to be used in the 2002 elections according to a provision in the Defense Authorization Act for FY2002 (P.L. 107-107), and it was expected that more states than the four that participated in 2000 would be involved. The provision called for the Secretary of Defense to "carry out a demonstration project under which absent uniformed services voters are permitted to cast ballots in the regularly scheduled general election for federal office for November 2002 through an electronic voting system" called the Secure Electronic Registration and Voting Experiment (SERVE).[38] But the law also included a provision under which the Secretary could delay the program until the 2004 general election if the Secretary determined that the demonstration project could "adversely affect the national security of the United States."[39] The law was signed by the President on December 28, 2001. Without sufficient time to develop the project before the 2002 election, the Secretary of Defense sent a letter to the Senate and House Armed Services Committees in May 2002 to request approval to implement the project for the 2004 election. In October 2002, staff from a number of congressional committees were briefed on the SERVE program, which was to provide the capability to identify and authenticate voters and local election officials using unique digital signatures. The voters and officials had to register with SERVE in order to be assigned the digital identity, which would allow them to access servers hosted by the FVAP in order to register and vote.[40] The program was expanded from four states that participated in the Voting Over the Internet project in 2000 to seven,[41] with a target of 100,000 participants.

The FVAP assembled a group in 2003, the Security Peer Review Group (SPRG), to review the SERVE program's security design. Several members of the group released their own, unofficial report in January 2004 that asserted that the program had fundamental security problems that made it vulnerable to "a variety of well-known cyber attacks (insider attacks, denial of service attacks, spoofing, automated vote buying, viral attacks on voter PCs, etc.), any one of which could be catastrophic."[42] As a result, the group recommended the following:

> Because the danger of successful, large-scale attacks is so great, we reluctantly recommend shutting down the development of SERVE immediately and not attempting anything like it in the future until both the Internet and the world's home computer infrastructure have been fundamentally redesigned, or some other unforeseen security breakthroughs appear.[43]

The Secretary of Defense subsequently suspended the program later in the year, and the defense authorization act for FY2005, enacted on October 28, 2004, instructed the Secretary to wait until the Election Assistance

Commission (EAC) issued guidelines for electronic absentee voting before pursuing another Internet voting project.[44] The EAC has not yet developed guidelines, but issued a report in April 2010 on its objectives and progress to date.[45]

Interim Voting Assistance System and Integrated Voting Alternative Site (IVAS)

DOD launched a new program in September 2004, apparently as a result of having to suspend the SERVE program, which allowed registered UOCAVA voters to request and receive absentee ballots over the Internet. Using the Interim Voting Assistance System (IVAS) website on an FVAP server, a previously registered voter in a state that volunteered to participate would request a ballot and the request would be forwarded to the appropriate election official. If the request was approved, the voter was notified by e-mail to retrieve the absentee ballot using the IVAS secure connection. The voter was required to download the ballot, print and complete it, then return it by mail to the local election official.

Under P.L. 109-234, the Emergency Supplemental Appropriations Act for Defense, the Global War on Terror, and Hurricane Recovery, 2006 (enacted on June 15, 2006), the Secretary of Defense was instructed to continue the IVAS program for uniformed services voters, their dependents, and Department of Defense personnel.[46] The Interim Voting Assistance System was subsequently reconfigured in September 2006, and the new system was called the Integrated Voting Alternative Site. It also required a voter to be previously registered and provided two means of requesting and receiving an absentee blank ballot: by e-mail or through a secure server. Both methods relied on a unique identifier that uniformed services personnel, their family members, and DOD overseas personnel and contractors possessed. To use the e-mail method, a previously registered voter would use the unique identifier to connect via the Internet to a tool on the FVAP website. The voter would complete an electronic version of the Federal Post Card Application (FPCA), save it as a PDF file (without an electronic or digital signature), and e-mail the attached file to their local election official for processing. The website included information from the FVAP's *Voting Assistance Guide* which provided information on each state's acceptable procedures for requesting and receiving absentee ballots (e-mail, facsimile, and postal mail) and local election official contact information. If the request was approved by the local official, a blank ballot was sent to the voter by whatever means the state allowed and the voter would complete and return the ballot. The second method required the voter to connect to a secure server using the unique identifier to complete an electronic version of the FPCA. A local election official would connect to the server to process the application and, if approved, post a PDF version of the blank ballot on the server. The voter would again connect to the server to access and print out the ballot. The voter could then complete and return the ballot to the election official. The IVAS system did not provide the means for the voter to return the completed ballot to the election official, but required the voter to send it by whatever means available in the particular voting jurisdiction (facsimile, e-mail, and postal mail).

Electronic Absentee Systems for Elections (EASE)

In May 2011, the Federal Voting Assistance Program announced a grants program to support research and development of electronic voting options for UOCAVA voters.[47] The program was designed to address the number one failure with respect to counting military and overseas citizen ballots: they were received by local election officials after the deadline for counting absentee ballots. The goal is that electronic innovations developed through the program will reduce the amount of time required by an individual to register to vote, send a ballot request, receive the ballot, and return it for counting. States, counties, cities, and townships are eligible to apply. Initially funded at $15.5 million, the amount disbursed to grants recipients was $25.4 million as of June 2012.[48] The program represents the first time the Department of Defense has offered grant assistance to election officials.

LEGISLATION

113th Congress

Six bills have been introduced that concern uniformed services and overseas voters. H.R. 12 and S. 123, which are identical, include provisions that would guarantee voting residency for family members of absent military personnel, require changes to reports on absentee ballot availability and transmission, revise the 45-day absentee ballot transmission rule, and permit the use of a single absentee ballot application for subsequent elections. H.R. 1655 would prohibit a state from certifying general election results until ballots from uniformed services voters had been counted. H.R. 2168 would require notification of the appropriate election official of a change of address for a service member who is deployed on active duty for more than 30 days or who has been redeployed, would repeal the waiver from the 45-day ballot availability deadline, would require express delivery for a failure to meet the deadline, would require establishing procedures to process military and overseas ballots in the event of a major disaster, and would prohibit a state from accepting a voter registration and absentee ballot application from an overseas voter because of early submission.

H.R. 3576 and S. 1728 are identical and

- would require states to submit a pre-election report on whether absentee ballots were sent by the 45-day deadline before an election;
- would repeal the waiver from the 45-day ballot availability deadline, would require express delivery for a failure to meet the deadline;
- would permit the use of a single absentee ballot application for subsequent elections;
- would prohibit a state from accepting a voter registration and absentee ballot application from an overseas voter because of early submission;
- would apply UOCAVA to the Northern Mariana Islands;
- would require a biennial report on the performance of the Federal Voting Assistance Program, to be reviewed by the Comptroller General with a report to the oversight committees for election years 2014 through 2020;
- would require providing active assistance to active duty members of the Armed Forces through an online system to facilitate voter registration, updating the voter registration record, and requesting an absentee ballot;
- would repeal the voting demonstration project authorized by the National Defense Authorization Act for FY2002; and
- would extend a guarantee of residency to family members of absent military personnel.

The Senate Committee on Rules and Administration held a hearing on S. 1728 on January 29, 2014.[49]

112th Congress

Five bills were introduced in the 112th Congress that would have affected UOCAVA voters. H.R. 702 would have amended UOCAVA to prohibit a state from certifying general election results until absentee ballots collected from uniformed services voters and delivered to election officials, as required by the MOVE Act amendments, had been counted. The bill would have delayed counting until the expiration of the 10-day period which begins on the date of the election or the date provided by state law, whichever is later. H.R. 5799 included provisions that would have guaranteed residency for voting to members of absent military personnel, amended UOCAVA to require express or electronic delivery of absentee ballots to voters if the state misses the 45 day ballot availability deadline, allowed for the use of a single absentee ballot application for all elections through the next general election, and applied UOCAVA to the Northern Mariana Islands. H.R. 5828 addressed a situation that resulted from the MOVE Act repeal of a provision of UOCAVA.[50] Before the repeal, a voter registration and absentee ballot application from a UOCAVA voter effectively covered all elections for two general election cycles, if the voter so desired. As a result, local election officials were required to mail ballots to the voter for all primary, primary run-off, and general elections. One consequence was that ballots were mailed to voters— particularly military voters—who were no longer at the address, creating an additional expense to local governments and inflating the number of ballots sent to, but not returned by, UOCAVA voters. H.R. 5828 would have permitted an absentee ballot application to be treated as an application for subsequent elections in the state through the next regular general election.

S. 331 would have ensured that military voters have the right to bring a civil action under the Uniformed and Overseas Citizens Absentee Voting Act to safeguard their right to vote. The National Defense Authorization Act for 2012, S. 1253, included a provision that would have amended UOCAVA to prohibit a state from refusing to process a valid voter registration or absentee ballot application from an overseas voter because it was submitted before the date on which the state begins accepting such applications for the year. This would have extended to civilian overseas voters the same protection currently provided to uniformed services voters by UOCAVA. Congress passed a version that originated in the House, H.R. 1540, which did not include such a provision. S. 3322 would have guaranteed residency for voting to members of absent military personnel, amended UOCAVA to require states to issue pre-election reports about the availability and timely transmission of absentee ballots, repealed the provision that allowed states to seek a waiver from transmission requirements, and established a private right of action with respect to the act.

On February 15, 2011, the Committee on House Administration held a hearing on the effectiveness of the MOVE Act in the 2010 election.[51]

111th Congress

A number of bills that focused on military and overseas voting were introduced in the 111th Congress. The Senate Rules Committee reported S. 1415, the Military and Overseas Citizens Voter Empowerment Act, as amended, on July 15, 2009. The text of the bill was subsequently added as an amendment to the National Defense Authorization Act for Fiscal Year 2010 (H.R. 2647), which was passed by the Senate on July 23. The House voted in favor of the conference report to the bill (H.Rept. 111-288) on October 8 and the Senate approved it on October 22; President Obama signed the bill on October 28 (P.L. 111-84). It established procedures for the use of e-mail and facsimile transmittal for registration and absentee ballot applications, established procedures for the collection of marked absentee ballots from overseas uniformed services voters for delivery to the appropriate state election officials, and established additional procedures and requirements to improve UOCAVA voting (see the section of this report entitled "Provisions of the Military and Overseas Voter Empowerment Act"). The House Administration Committee also reported H.R. 2393, the Military Voting Protection Act, on June 10, 2009. The bill would have required the Secretary of Defense to establish procedures for the collection of marked absentee ballots from overseas uniformed services voters for delivery to the appropriate state election officials; the new law, P.L. 111-84, includes a similar provision. Both the Senate Rules and Administration and House Administration Committees had previously held hearings on UOCAVA voting. The hearings were convened on May 13 in the Senate and May 21 in the House.

Other bills introduced in the 111th Congress included two sponsored by Representative Maloney, H.R. 1659 and H.R. 1739. The first would have amended UOCAVA to require that the presidential designee have experience in election administration that includes oversight of voter registration and absentee ballot distribution, and it would have established an Overseas Voting Advisory Board. H.R. 1739 was a more far-reaching proposal that would have amended UOCAVA to make a series of adjustments concerning balloting materials and related election administration procedures in the states, and would have established a grant program for voter outreach. H.R. 2082 would have amended UOCAVA to require states to accept ballots submitted by overseas voters using a provider of express mail service, as long as the ballot was submitted no later than the day before, and received within 10 days after, the election. The bill would also have required the presidential designee to reimburse the voter for the express mail cost. As noted above, H.R. 2393 would have amended UOCAVA to require the presidential designee to collect marked general election ballots from overseas uniformed services voters for delivery to the appropriate election officials before the polls close, using U.S. Postal Service express mail delivery. The bill would also have required a tracking system so the voter could determine whether the ballot was delivered. It was reported by the House Administration Committee on June 10. A companion measure, S. 1026, was introduced in the Senate. Finally, H.R. 2823 would have required states to accept and process any otherwise valid voter registration application without any requirement for notarization and would have permitted electronic submission of the official post card form to register and request an absentee ballot.

110th Congress

Several relevant election reform bills were introduced in the 110th Congress, and two were acted on. On October 1, 2008, the Senate passed S. 3073, which would have required the Secretary of Defense to collect ballots from overseas military voters and ensure their delivery to election officials using express mail services. On the House side, H.R. 6625 was passed on September 17, 2008; it would have allowed state election officials to designate facilities of the Department of Veterans Affairs as voter registration agencies under the National Voter Registration Act (P.L. 103-31, the "motor-voter" law).

Other bills that were not acted on included H.R. 2835, H.R. 4173, H.R. 4237, H.R. 5673, and S. 1487. H.R. 2835 would have extended UOCAVA law's provisions to cover legislative and gubernatorial elections in American Samoa. H.R. 4173 would have prohibited states from requiring notarization of absentee ballots, broadened the use of the federal write-in ballot, established a grant program to inform overseas citizens about absentee voting, and required that overseas federal employees be informed about UOCAVA and information about the law included in U.S. passports. H.R. 4237 would have prohibited states from refusing to accept registration or ballot applications because they do not meet nonessential requirements, clarified postage markings on balloting materials, and would have amended the law concerning individuals who never lived in the United States, notification of the rejection of registration or ballot applications, and the use of the diplomatic pouch to transmit absentee ballots. H.R. 5673 would have required the Secretary of Defense to collect marked absentee ballots from overseas uniformed services voters and to guarantee their delivery to the appropriate election officials before the polls close. The bill would also have encouraged the use of private providers of air transportation to deliver ballots, which would allow individual voters to track the progress of their voted ballot. S. 1487 would have prohibited states from refusing to accept registration or ballot applications because they do not meet nonessential requirements and would have permitted accepting a federal write-in ballot from an overseas voter if it is submitted from a location in the United States.

REPORTS ON UOCAVA VOTING AND EFFECTIVENESS, 2006-2012

2012 Election

In July 2012 the Election Assistance Commission issued its biennial report on voting by members of the uniformed services and overseas citizens.[52] The states transmitted 876,362 ballots to UOCAVA voters for the 2012 general election, of which 606,425 were returned for counting. The disposition of the 270,000 unreturned ballots is unknown, because states "often lack the ability of resources to track transmitted ballots that are not returned."[53] States counted 95.8% of returned ballots,[54] an improvement over the 93.6% that were counted in the 2008 election.[55] Most of the ballots that were rejected—40.4%—were returned too late to be counted, while others were rejected because there was a problem with the voter signature, or the ballot lacked a postmark, or for some other reason.

Ballots were transmitted from all 50 states, the District of Columbia, American Samoa, Guam, and Puerto Rico, although more than half (456,363) were sent from seven states: California, Florida, New York, Pennsylvania, Texas, Virginia, and Washington. The report included numerous tables that provided detailed information by state for both uniformed services and overseas civilian voters, including statistics on transmitted ballots, ballots submitted for counting, rejected ballots by reason, and the number of counted ballots.

The report was the fifth undertaken by the EAC since it was established in 2003. It noted that "[t]he quality of information regarding UOCAVA ballots continues to improve, and the 2012 survey data yielded a more complete picture of UOCAVA balloting than past surveys. States are generally making significant strides in designing their data management systems to produce the necessary data on UOCAVA voters. Gaps in State tracking of UOCAVA voters remain, however, and continued attention to data collection on UOCAVA voters and their ballots is needed."[56]

The Overseas Vote Foundation (OVF) issued its biennial election report in January 2013.[57] The report for 2012 was based on post-election surveys that relied on OVF contact lists for UOCAVA voters, local election officials (LEOs), and domestic voters on the mailing list for OVF's newly launched U.S. Vote Foundation to facilitate absentee voting in the states.

Among its findings the report noted that 34.9% of UOCAVA voters used an electronic method to submit the registration and ballot request form in comparison to 23% in 2010 and 18% in 2008. The MOVE Act of 2009 required that states adopt at least one electronic method to facilitate registration and requesting a ballot. With respect to receiving a ballot, those who sent the form by postal method fared slightly better (85.6% received a ballot) than those who submitted the form electronically (81.3%). Most voters returned the marked ballot by regular mail (63.3%), while 14.9% returned it by electronic means (fax, email, or uploading to an election website). From the perspective of election officials, the leading reasons for rejecting a registration and ballot request was that it arrived after the deadline (27.5%), it lacked a signature or date (19.3%), or it was incomplete (14.5%). Of the various electronic methods states used to transmit blank ballots, most were sent as a PDF attachment by email (90.5%). The use of electronic methods for transmission also introduced new problems, however. Among the problems encountered when using electronic means of transmission, LEOs reported that 53.4% of voters who had problems said they did not receive the ballot and 31.9% were unable to open the PDF files.

2010 Election

The Inspector General of the Department of Defense issued a report on August 31, 2012, that assessed implementation of the MOVE Act by the Federal Voting Assistance Program.[58] To determine whether UOCAVA voting assistance programs have been effective, the report assessed the most recent

FVAP report to Congress in 2010 (discussed in detail below) and whether the MOVE Act requirement to establish voting assistance offices on all military installations was accomplished. FVAP's survey on military voting in 2010 was based on a 15% response rate, which the report noted should be improved.

The main focus of the report was the MOVE Act imperative to establish a voting assistance office at every military installation worldwide, except for those in a warzone. Based on an attempt to contact the 224 installation voting assistance offices (IVAOs) listed on the FVAP website, the report authors noted that "about half the time, we were unable to contact the IVAOs the website identified."[59] The report concluded that not all IVAOs had been established as required because no additional funding was provided for the initiative, estimated to cost in excess of $15 million-$20 million a year. As a solution, the report recommended that FVAP and the Under Secretary of Defense for Personnel and Readiness draft a legislative proposal to request relief from the MOVE Act requirement and to permit the Secretaries of the Military Departments to use their discretion in designating the IVAOs, with "the intent that the Services optimize voting assistance to military personnel and other overseas citizens."[60]

The Military Voter Protection Project (MVPP) issued a report in August 2012 that also discussed incomplete implementation of MOVE Act provisions and cited, as a consequence, the low number of absentee ballot requests from military voters in selected states.[61] According to the report, the MOVE Act should have increased a voter's opportunity to request an absentee ballot, but "the 2012 pre-election data shows a remarkable decrease in such requests from military voters, especially when that data is compared to data from 2008."[62] The report notes that the number of absentee ballot requests will increase in the lead-up to the election, but the number needed to reach 2008 levels is "staggering."

On October 11, 2011, the Election Assistance Commission issued its fourth report to Congress on the number of ballots sent to and received by those persons covered by the UOCAVA.[63] The Federal Voting Assistance Program (FVAP) also provides a regular report to Congress and the President on UOCAVA voting; the report that presented information on the 2010 election was issued on October 18, 2011.[64] It was the first of these reports to cover a non-presidential general election, as mandated by MOVE Act changes to the UOCAVA in 2009. FVAP's previous 18 reports were issued following a presidential election.[65]

The EAC report noted that states counted 93% of UOCAVA ballots that were submitted, a similar figure to what was reported in 2008. Of these, 49%

were from uniformed services voters and 41% were from overseas civilians, with the rest identified as "other" or "non-categorized." States transmitted 611,058 ballots, of which 211,749 were submitted for counting and 197,390 were counted. As stated in the report, "[t]he fate of the approximately 400,000 remaining ballots is difficult to discern; unless ballots are returned as undeliverable or spoiled, which accounted for nearly an additional 47,000 ballots, States often lack the ability or resources to track them."[66] The most common reason for rejecting a returned ballot was that it was not received by the election official on time. Thirty-two percent of ballots were rejected for this reason. Finally, the report noted a drop in the number of ballots transmitted to UOCAVA voters between 2008 and 2010, from 989,208 to 611,058, which might be expected when presidential and non-presidential election participation is compared.

The FVAP report was based on post-election surveys of active duty military voters, their spouses, overseas citizens, voting assistance officers in DOD and the Department of State, and local election officials. The FVAP adjusted the survey results for members of the active duty military (ADM) because the ADM is "more male and a much younger population than the overall citizen voting population," and both groups participate at lower rates than other groups in the voting population, which "drives down the voter participation rates of the military, all other things being equal."[67] The adjusted results "allow for a direct comparison to the general voting population." The report noted that 85% of ADM were registered, in comparison to 65% of the civilian voting age population (CVAP). In terms of voter turnout, 45.5% of ADM voted, as compared to 46% of the CVAP. Data for overseas citizens are difficult to obtain because the number of overseas citizens is unknown and a random sample cannot be obtained. However, according to the responses of local election officials who were surveyed (53% of 7,296 total jurisdictions), 45% of registered overseas citizens voted in the election. Finally, the report noted that ADM voter registration was virtually the same for 2008 and 2010 (both non-presidential elections), while a 21% increase in the *unadjusted* voter participation rate from 2006 to 2010 "may indicate that the 45-day prior ballot transmission, electronic ballot transmission, and expedited ballot return of overseas military ballot requirements of the MOVE Act have substantially improved the opportunity for active duty military voters to successfully cast a ballot."[68]

The Overseas Vote Foundation issued its report on the 2010 election on February 10, 2011, which found that 18% of UOCAVA voters in the survey reported that they did not receive a requested ballot and another 16.5%

reported that they had received the ballot "late."[69] The report was based on two separate surveys of 5,257 self-selected UOCAVA voters and 1,555 local election officials.[70] Among its results, the survey found that 18% of voters did not receive a ballot and 16.5% of respondents received their ballot after the middle of October. With respect to the MOVE Act's requirement for electronic transmission of registration and ballot applications and blank ballots, the survey found that 80% of respondents used an electronic means to send an application, and 23% received a blank ballot electronically.[71]

2008 Election

The Overseas Vote Foundation published a report in February 2009 based on survey responses from approximately 24,000 UOCAVA voters and 1,000 local election officials. The report noted that there is "some evidence of overall progress" with respect to voting under UOCAVA, but that "progress is uneven, and the surveys point to numerous areas ripe for reform."[72] For example, one in four respondents did not receive their requested absentee ballot; 8% of these voters used the federal write-in absentee ballot to vote, but 14% did not participate in the election (not all voters are aware that they may use the federal write-in ballot if they have requested a regular state ballot that does not arrive). Furthermore, more than half (52%) of those who tried to vote but failed to do so either received a late ballot or never received one at all.[73]

The Pew Center on the States issued a January 2009 report that examined the variety of state practices that can make casting a ballot difficult for UOCAVA voters and made recommendations for improving the voting process.[74] Among its findings, the report noted that "25 states and Washington, D.C., need to improve their absentee balloting rules for military voters abroad," and "the other 25 states would better serve these voters by giving them additional time to request and return their ballots as well."[75] The report recommended eliminating notarization requirements, expanding electronic transmission of election materials, expanding the use of the federal blank ballot if a regular ballot does not arrive in time, and providing for a period of at least 45 days to receive and return a ballot.

In October 2007, the Overseas Vote Foundation first launched its website to assist UOCAVA voters by providing a means to electronically register and request a ballot.[76] The OVF, a nonpartisan, non-governmental entity, offered the necessary information to complete the application process for each of the states, including a database of local election officials to whom the applications would be delivered.

2006 Election

Reports on military and overseas voting in the 2006 election highlighted continuing challenges faced by these voters, despite efforts in the previous several years to improve voting rates. The GAO issued an evaluation of federal efforts to facilitate electronic absentee voting in June 2007,[77] and the EAC reported in September 2007 the results of its survey of military and overseas voters after the 2006 election.[78] According to the EAC report, 33% of ballots requested by these voters were cast or counted in the election; of those that were not counted, nearly 70% were returned to election officials as undeliverable. GAO estimated that there were 6 million UOCAVA voters, and its report outlined a series of recommendations to DOD (the FVAP) and the EAC for electronic solutions to overcome the obstacles posed by time and distance.

CONCLUSION

The inherent difficulties in ensuring the voting rights of Americans scattered around the world, particularly those on active duty in the Armed Forces during wartime, have resulted in frequent revisions to applicable voting laws. Congress has been especially vigilant in recent years, amending the current law—the Uniformed and Overseas Citizens Absentee Voting Act of 1986— six times since 2001. It is the only area of election administration law in which legislation has been enacted since passage of the Help America Vote Act of 2002 (P.L. 107-252).

Based on military and overseas citizen voting participation in the 2012 election as reported by the Election Assistance Commission, further improvements to the law might be considered in the 113th Congress. The states counted nearly 96% of ballots that were returned in the election, yet 31% of the ballots requested by and sent to UOCAVA voters were not returned to the states for counting. In contrast, 16% of domestic absentee ballots transmitted were not returned for counting.[79] Such disparities provide an incentive to seek further improvements for UOCAVA voters and Congress has shown an abiding willingness to do so.

End Notes

[1] R. Michael Alvarez, Thad E. Hall, and Brian F. Roberts, *Military Voting and the Law: Procedural and Technological Solutions to the Ballot Transit Problem*, CALTECH/MIT Voting Technology Project, VTP Working Paper #53, Pasadena, CA and Cambridge, MA, March 2007, pp. 12-14.

[2] U.S. Department of Defense, Office of the Assistant Secretary of Defense (Public Affairs), *The Federal Voting Assistance Program, Eleventh Report*, December 1977, p. 2.

[3] Boyd A. Martin, "The Service Vote in the Elections of 1944," *The American Political Science Review*, vol. 39, no. 4 (August 1945), p. 722.

[4] Ibid.

[5] U.S. Department of Defense, *The Federal Voting Assistance Program*, 11th Report (Washington: December 1977), p. 2.

[6] "Should Soldiers Have the Vote?," *Newsweek*, December, 1943, pp. 54, 59.

[7] P.L. 77-712, §1.

[8] 42 U.S.C. §1973ff.

[9] §107. The uniformed services include members of the Merchant Marine, Army, Navy, Air Force, Marine Corps, Coast Guard, the commissioned corps of the Public Health Service, and the commissioned corps of the National Oceanic and Atmospheric Administration.

[10] §107 (1). An absent uniformed services voter is defined as follows: a member of a uniformed service on active duty or a member of the merchant marine who, by reason of such active duty or service in the merchant marine, is absent from the place of residence where the member is otherwise qualified to vote; and a spouse or dependent of a member of a uniformed service or a member of the merchant marine who is absent from his or her place of residence where he or she is otherwise qualified to vote, because of the active duty or service of the member.

[11] 42 U.S.C. §1973ff-1(1), as amended by §1606 (b) of the National Defense Authorization Act of 2002, by §704 of the Help America Vote Act of 2002, and by §592 of the National Defense Authorization Act for FY2010.

[12] 42 U.S.C. §1973ff-1(2), as amended by §707 of the Help America Vote Act of 2002.

[13] 42 U.S.C. §1973ff-1(3).

[14] The United States Postal Service domestic mail manual notes that "To be mailable without prepayment of postage, the balloting materials must be deposited at a U.S. post office, an overseas U.S. military post office, or an American Embassy or American Consulate." The relevant section of the manual may be found under "Absentee Balloting Materials" at http://pe.usps.com/text/dmm300/703.htm#wp1140123.

[15] 42 U.S.C. §1973ff-3.

[16] The following states passed legislation to comply with the MOVE Act: Arizona, Florida, Georgia, Hawaii, Idaho, Illinois, Indiana, Iowa, Louisiana, Maine, Michigan, Minnesota, Missouri, Mississippi, Nebraska, New Hampshire, New York, Ohio, Oklahoma, South Dakota, Tennessee, Utah, Virginia, and West Virginia.

[17] U.S. Department of Defense, Office of the Assistant Secretary of Defense, "DOD Announces Military and Overseas Voting Waivers," No. 775-10, August 27, 2010, which is available at http://www.defense.gov/utility/printitem.aspx?
print=http://www.defense.gov/releases/release.aspx?releaseid=13837.

[18] The Associated Press State & Local Wire, "Judge extends deadline for military ballots," October 30, 2010, which may be found at http://www.abc2news.com/dpp/news/region/anne_arundel_county_/judge-extends-military-ballotdeadline.

[19] FOXNews.com, "DOJ Responds to Accusation of Stalling on MOVE Act for Voters in Military," August 4, 2010, available at http://www.foxnews.com/politics.

[20] U.S. Department of Justice press release, *Justice Department Reaches Agreement to Protect Rights of Military and Overseas Voters in Wisconsin*, September 10, 2010, which may be found at http://www.justice.gov/opa/pr/2010/ September/10-crt-1018.html.

[21] U.S. Department of Justice press release, *Justice Department Announces Lawsuit to Protect Rights of Military and Overseas Voters in Guam*, October 6, 2010, which may be found at http://www.justice.gov/opa/pr/2010/October/10-crt1122.html.

[22] *The Seattle Times*, "Feds: 65,000 Overseas Voters Protected Before Vote", October 27, 2010, which may be found at http://seattletimes.nwsource.com/html /politics.

[23] U.S. Department of Justice press release, *Justice Department Reaches Agreement to Protect Rights of Military and Overseas Voters in New Mexico*, October 13, 2010, which may be found at http://www.justice.gov/opa/pr/2010/ October/10-crt-1137.html.

[24] The consent decree may be found at http://www.fvap.gov/resources.

[25] The consent decree may be found at http://www.fvap.gov/resources.

[26] The memorandum of agreement for Alaska may be found at http://www.fvap.gov /resources ak_doj_agreement.pdf.

[27] The memorandum of agreement for Colorado may be found at http://www.fvap.gov /resources co_doj_agreement.pdf.

[28] The memorandum of agreement for the District of Columbia may be found at http://www.fvap.gov/resources dc_doj_agreement.pdf.

[29] The memorandum of agreement for Hawaii may be found at http://www.fvap.gov/resources hi_doj_agreement.pdf.

[30] U.S. Department of Justice press release, *Justice Department Reached Agreements to Protect Rights of Military and Overseas Voters From New York, Kansas and Mississippi*, October 15, 2010, which may be found at http://www.justice.gov/opa/pr/2010/October/10-crt-1158.html.

[31] Ibid.

[32] U.S. Department of Justice press release, *Department Announces Agreement to Protect Rights of Military and Overseas Voters from Nevada*, October 8, 2010, which may be found at http://www.justice.gov/opa/pr/2010/October/ 10-crt-1130.html.

[33] The memorandum of agreement for the Virgin Islands may be found at http://www.fvap.gov /resources vi_doj_aggreement.pdf.

[34] Information on individual state rules can be found in the Federal Voting Assistance Program's *Voting Assistance Guide*, although changes to procedures in recent months may not be accounted for in the *Guide*, which may be found at http://www.fvap.gov/resources.

[35] The report may be found at http://www.justice.gov/crt/about/vot/misc/move_act_report.pdf.

[36] Because of possible tax liability incurred in some states based on legal residence, the *Guide* advises members of the military to consult a Judge Advocate General officer or legal counsel before changing residence (to the state or territory where they are stationed, for example); Federal Voting Assistance Program, *Voting Assistance Guide, 2014-2015*, Washington, D.C., September 2013, p. 474, http://www.fvap.gov/uploads/FVAP /States/vag2014.pdf.

[37] Department of Defense, Washington Headquarters Services, Federal Voting Assistance Program, "Voting Over the Internet Pilot Project Assessment Report," June 2001, p. ES-2.

[38] §1604 (a)(1).

[39] §1604 (a)(2).

[40] A description of the program may be found in a report by Andrew Regenscheid and Nelson Hastings, *A Threat Analysis on UOCAVA Voting Systems*, NISTIR 7551 (National Institute of Standards and Technology, December 2008), pp. 5-6, available at http://www.nist.gov/itl/vote

[41] Arkansas, Florida, Hawaii, North Carolina, South Carolina, Utah, and Washington, as reported in an undated internal document entitled "Secure Electronic Registration and Voting Experiment," pp. 6-7, available from the Federal Voting Assistance Program at http://www.fvap.gov/resources

[42] Dr. David Jefferson, Dr. Aviel D. Rubin, Dr. Barbara Simons, Dr. David Wagner, "A Security Analysis of the Secure Electronic Registration and Voting Experiment (SERVE)," p. 2, available at http://servesecurityreport.org/.

[43] Ibid., p. 3.

[44] Section 567 of P.L. 108-375, The Ronald W. Reagan National Defense Authorization Act for Fiscal Year 2005, instructed the Secretary to suspend the electronic voting demonstration project "until the first regularly scheduled general election for Federal office which occurs after the Election Assistance Commission notifies the Secretary that the Commission has established electronic absentee voting guidelines and certifies that it will assist the Secretary in carrying out the project."

[45] Election Assistance Commission, "Report to Congress on EAC's Efforts to Establish Guidelines for Remote Electronic Absentee Voting Systems," April 26, 2010, which may be found at http://www.fvap.gov/resources eacroadmap.pdf.

[46] Section 1212 (b)(1) said, "The Interim Voting Assistance System (IVAS) Ballot Request Program shall be continued with respect to all absent uniformed services voters, Department of Defense personnel, and dependents covered by the Uniformed and Overseas Citizens Absentee Voting Act (42 U.S.C. 1973ff et seq.) with the objective to further improve ballot request procedures and voting assistance with respect to such persons."

[47] U.S. Department of Defense, Federal Voting Assistance Program, "DoD Announces Grants Program to Ease Voting Process," press release, May 19, 2011.

[48] U.S. Department of Defense, Federal Voting Assistance Program, "DoD Awards Grants for State & Local Military/Overseas Voting Systems," press release, June 21, 2012.

[49] The hearing can be found at http://www.rules ContentRecord_id=e07caaca-5d57-4ffc-8257-7bdb82c99a0e& ContentType_id=14f995b9-dfa5-407a-9d35- 56cc7152a7ed&Group_id=1983a2a8-4fc3-4062-a50e-7997351c154b.

[50] Representative Carolyn Maloney, "Rep. Maloney Introduces Bill to Help Eliminate Uncertainty in Absentee Ballot Process for Americans Abroad," press release, May 18, 2012.

[51] Witness testimony may be found at http://cha.house.gov/index.php?option=com_content&task=view&id=363& Itemid=381.

[52] U.S. Election Assistance Commission, *Uniformed and Overseas Citizens Absentee Voting Act: Survey Findings*, Washington, July 2013, at http://www.eac.gov/assets.

[53] Ibid., p. 9.

[54] Ibid., p. 1.

[55] U.S. Election Assistance Commission, *Uniformed and Overseas Citizens Absentee Voting*, Uniformed and Overseas Citizens Absentee Voting Act: Survey Findings, Washington, November 2009, p. 2.

[56] Ibid., p. 9.

[57] Overseas Vote Foundation, "OVF and US Vote 2012 Post-Election Survey Report," at https://www.overseasvotefoundation.org/files/OVF_ElectionReport_2013_web.

[58] Inspector General United States Department of Defense, *Assessment of the Federal Voting Assistance Program Office Implementation of the Military and Overseas Voter Empowerment Act*, Report No. DODIG-2012-123, August 31, 2012, at http://www.dodig.mil/SPO/Reports/DODIG-2012-123.pdf.

[59] U.S. Department of Defense, Federal Voting Assistance Program, "2010 Post Election Survey Report to Congress," September, 2011, p. 12, at http://www.fvap.gov/resources.

[60] Ibid., p. ii.

[61] Military Voter Protection Project, "Military Voting Update: A Bleak Picture in 2012," August 21, 2012, at http://mvpproject.org/wp-content/uploads/2012/08/Bleak-Picture-for-Military-Voters.pdf.

[62] Ibid., p.

[63] U.S. Election Assistance Commission, "Uniformed and Overseas Citizens Absentee Voting Act: Survey Observations," October 2011, at http://www.eac.gov/assets EAC%202010%20UOCAVA%20Report_FINAL.pdf.

[64] U.S. Department of Defense, Federal Voting Assistance Program, "2010 Post Election Survey Report to Congress," September, 2011.

[65] Ibid., p. 2.

[66] U.S. Election Assistance Commission, "Uniformed and Overseas Citizens," p. 9.

[67] U.S. Department of Defense, "2010 Post Election Survey," p. ii.

[68] Ibid., p. vi.

[69] Overseas Vote Foundation, "Moving Forward: 2010 OVF Post Election UOCAVA Survey Report and Analysis," February 2011, p. 2, at https://www.overseasvotefoundation.org/files/OVF_2010_Post_Election_Survey_Report.pdf.

[70] The OVF sent an online invitation to complete the survey to 89,322 UOCAVA voters on the OVF mailing list, of which 4,913 responded. The survey was made available to any overseas voter via an open URL and an additional 344 voters completed the survey in this manner. Respondents were from 140 different countries and all states (but none of the territories). The survey of UOCAVA voters was conducted from November 2 to December 31, 2010. The local election officials survey was conducted from November 30, 2010, to January 1, 2011, and was sent to 10,712 officials in the 50 states, the District of Columbia, American Samoa, Guam, Puerto Rico, and the Virgin Islands; there were 1,555 respondents.

[71] The Overseas Vote Foundation, "Moving Forward," p. 2.

[72] The Overseas Vote Foundation, "2008 OVF Post Election UOCAVA Survey Report and Analysis: A Detailed Look at How Overseas and Military Voters and Election Officials Fared in the 2008 General Election and What To Do About It," February 2009, at https://www.overseasvotefoundation.org/files/OVF_2009_PostElectionSurvey_Report.pdf.

[73] Ibid., p. 5.

[74] The Pew Center on the States, *No Time to Vote: Challenges Facing America's Overseas Military Voters*, January, 2009, at http://www.pewtrusts.org/uploadedFiles/wwwpewtrustsorg/Reports/Election_reform.

[75] Ibid.

[76] The OVF website at https://www.overseasvotefoundation.org/overseas/home.htm.

[77] The GAO report may be found at http://www.gao.gov/new.items/d07774.pdf.

[78] The EAC report may be found at http://www.eac.gov/clearinghouse/2006-uniformed-and-overseas-citizens-votingact-survey-and-conference.

[79] U.S. Election Assistance Commission, *2012 Election Administration and Voting Survey: A Summary of Key Findings*, Washington, D.C., September 2013, pp. 35-36, at http://www.eac.gov/assets 050%20EAC%20VoterSurvey_508Compliant.pdf.

INDEX